Neurolaw and Criminal Jurisprudence in India

This work explores the transformative potential of neuroscience in reshaping India's criminal justice system. It deftly navigates the complex terrain of neurolaw, examining its implications for criminal responsibility, rehabilitation, and the very foundations of legal thought. Drawing on cutting-edge neuroscientific research and India's rich philosophical traditions, the work proposes innovative approaches to longstanding legal and ethical dilemmas. It covers a wide range of topics with depth and nuance, from a neurocriminological audit of Indian criminal codes to an exploration of neuroplasticity in offender rehabilitation. It includes a fascinating case study of the Vipassana meditation program in Indian prisons, illustrating the practical applications of neurolaw principles. The volume promises to spark crucial conversations about the nature of human behavior, the purpose of punishment, and the possibility of a more humane and effective justice system. It is a bold step toward a neuroscience-informed jurisprudence that honors both scientific truth and human dignity. At the intersection of neuroscience, law, and Indian philosophy, the work offers a unique perspective on some of the most pressing questions in modern jurisprudence. Representing a significant contribution to the global discourse on neurolaw and offering concrete suggestions for legal reform, judicial practice, and policymaking, it will be an essential read for legal scholars, neuroscientists, policymakers, and anyone interested in the future of criminal justice.

Dr. Pragya Mishra is Assistant Professor in Law at the University of Allahabad, Prayagraj, India.

Neurolaw and Criminal Jurisprudence in India

Pragya Mishra

LONDON AND NEW YORK

First published 2025
by Routledge
4 Park Square, Milton Park, Abingdon, Oxon OX14 4RN

and by Routledge
605 Third Avenue, New York, NY 10158

Routledge is an imprint of the Taylor & Francis Group, an informa business

© 2025 Pragya Mishra

The right of Pragya Mishra to be identified as author of this work has been asserted in accordance with sections 77 and 78 of the Copyright, Designs and Patents Act 1988.

All rights reserved. No part of this book may be reprinted or reproduced or utilised in any form or by any electronic, mechanical, or other means, now known or hereafter invented, including photocopying and recording, or in any information storage or retrieval system, without permission in writing from the publishers.

Trademark notice: Product or corporate names may be trademarks or registered trademarks, and are used only for identification and explanation without intent to infringe.

British Library Cataloguing-in-Publication Data
A catalogue record for this book is available from the British Library

ISBN: 978-1-032-93993-3 (hbk)
ISBN: 978-1-032-93736-6 (pbk)
ISBN: 978-1-003-56739-4 (ebk)

DOI: 10.4324/9781003567394

Typeset in Times New Roman
by Apex CoVantage, LLC

Contents

Preface ix
Acknowledgments xi
About the Author xiii

1 Introduction: Neurolaw's Global Emergence and India's Unique Position 1
Rise of Neurolaw as an Interdisciplinary Field 1
Current State and Key Challenges of Neurolaw in the Indian Context 2
Neuroscientific Evidence in Indian Courts: Potential and Limitations 2
Bharatiya Nyaya Sanhita and Neurolaw: A New Legal Landscape 3
Neuroscience and Indian Philosophical Traditions: A Synergistic Approach 5
Neurolaw and Mental Health in India 8
Challenges and Ethical Considerations in Neurolaw 9
Global Context: India's Potential Contributions to Neurolaw 10
Structure of the Book 12
Conclusion: Toward a Neurojuridical Renaissance in India 12

2 Foundations of Neurolaw and Neurocriminology 15
Key Concepts in Neuroscience Relevant to Law 15
Neurobiology of Criminal Behavior 15
Implications for Criminal Justice Systems Globally and in India 21

3 Neurocriminological Audit of Indian Criminal Codes   26
Analysis of the Bharatiya Nyaya Sanhita through a Neuroscientific Lens 26
Comparative Analysis with International Approaches 32
Proposed Reforms Based on Neuroscientific Insights 35
Case Studies from Indian Courts 39

4 Reimagining Sentencing: Case for Rehabilitative and Restorative Justice   42
Introduction 42
Critique of Current Sentencing Practices in India and Abroad 43
Neuroscience-Informed Rehabilitative Justice Models 45
Restorative Justice Principles and Their Neuroscientific Basis 48
Implementing Neuroscience-Informed Sentencing in India 51
Ethical Considerations and Potential Challenges 52

5 Restorative Justice and Neurolaw: A Mindfulness-Based Approach   55
Understanding Neuroplasticity: The Brain's Remarkable Ability to Change 55
Implications for Offender Rehabilitation 57
Potential Applications in the Indian Context 59
Traditional Indian Practices and Neuroplasticity 61
Case Studies and Evidence 64
Challenges and Ethical Considerations 65
Future Directions 67

6 Case Study: The Vipassana Prison Meditation Program   69
Introduction 69
Vipassana Meditation Technique: An Overview 69
Theoretical Framework: Vipassana and Neurocriminology 70
Implementation of Vipassana in Prison Settings 72
Empirical Outcomes and Research Findings 74
Theoretical Implications: Revisiting Free Will and Responsibility 76

Challenges and Ethical Considerations 78
Future Directions and Policy Implications 79

7 **Metaphysics of Neurolaw: Free Will, Determinism, and Criminal Responsibility**   83
  Neuroscientific Challenges to Traditional Notions of Free Will 83
  Implications for Criminal Responsibility 85
  Toward a Neuroscience-Informed Philosophy of Law in India 87
  Indian Philosophical Perspectives on Free Will and Determinism 91
  Neuroscience and Restorative Justice 94
  Neurolaw and Mental Health 95
  Neurolaw and Juvenile Justice 97
  Neurolaw and Legal Education 98

8 **Neurolaw and Mental Health Legislation in India**   100
  Analysis of India's Mental Health Laws from a Neurolaw Perspective 100
  Proposed Neuroscience-Informed Reforms 103
  Comparative Analysis with International Approaches 105
  Implementation Challenges and Strategies 110

9 **Neurotechnology and the Future of Criminal Justice: India and Beyond**   113
  Emerging Neurotechnologies and Their Potential Applications 113
  Ethical and Legal Challenges in the Indian and Global Context 116
  Developing a Regulatory Framework for Neurotechnology in Criminal Justice 118
  India's Potential Contributions to Global Neurolaw 122

10 **Toward an Indian Neurojuridical Ontology: India's Contributions to Global Neurolaw**   127
  Synthesis of Key Insights 127
  A Distinctly Indian Approach to Neurolaw 129

India's Potential Contributions to Global Neurolaw Discourse 132
Challenges and Future Directions 135
A Call to Action 136

Glossary	*138*
Appendices	*139*
Bibliography	*143*
Index	*144*

Preface

In the corridors of India's courtrooms and the laboratories of its neuroscience research centers, a quiet revolution is unfolding. The convergence of neuroscience and law – a field known as neurolaw – is challenging our fundamental understanding of criminality, justice, and human behavior. As an academic straddling these two worlds, I have watched with fascination as this interdisciplinary field has evolved, promising to reshape the very foundations of our criminal justice system.

This book *Neurolaw and Criminal Jurisprudence in India* is born out of half a decade of research, contemplation, and dialogue at this exciting intersection. It is an attempt to chart the contours of a uniquely Indian approach to neurolaw, one that draws on our rich cultural and philosophical heritage while embracing cutting-edge scientific insights.

The journey that led to this book began in the halls of the National Law University, Delhi, where I, as a doctoral candidate, first encountered the provocative questions posed by neuroscience to our legal assumptions. It continued through my doctoral research, where I delved deep into the neuroscientific underpinnings of criminal behavior and the ethical implications of brain-based interventions in the justice system. My experiences teaching law students and engaging with legal practitioners further underscored the urgent need for a comprehensive exploration of neurolaw in the Indian context.

Throughout this journey, I have been struck by the transformative potential of neurolaw. From the innovative use of meditation in prisons to the development of brain-based rehabilitation programs, India is uniquely positioned to pioneer a holistic and humane approach to criminal justice. At the same time, I have grappled with the profound ethical and philosophical questions raised by these advances. How do we reconcile our growing understanding of the brain's role in behavior with our cherished notions of free will and moral responsibility? How can we harness the power of neuroscience to create a more just and compassionate society without compromising individual rights and dignity?

This book does not pretend to have all the answers. Instead, it aims to spark a crucial conversation about the future of criminal justice in India in the age of neuroscience. It is an invitation to legal scholars, neuroscientists, policymakers, and engaged citizens to reimagine our approach to crime, punishment, and rehabilitation in light of our evolving understanding of the human brain.

As we stand on the cusp of this neurojuridical renaissance, it is my hope that this book will serve as a roadmap for navigating the challenges and opportunities ahead. May it contribute to the development of a criminal justice system, not just in India but globally, that is not only more effective and scientifically grounded but also more humane, just, and aligned with the highest ideals of our democratic society.

Dr. Pragya Mishra
Prayagraj

Acknowledgments

As this book finds its way into the world, I am filled with profound gratitude for all those who have contributed to its creation. This work is a testament to the collective wisdom, support, and inspiration of many.

First, I bow my head in deep gratitude to the Almighty, for the ever-present divine grace that has guided this endeavor. May we all strive to realize the eternal flame of truth that resides within each of us.

I want to express my deepest appreciation to the editorial team at **Routledge Taylor & Francis**. My heartfelt thanks especially to **Ms. Medha Malviya**, who onboarded me for this project and saw its potential from the very beginning. Your initial faith in this work set the foundation for everything that followed.

A special note of gratitude goes to **Ms. Alison Kirk** and **Ms. Anna Gallagher**, my editors at Routledge. Anna, your dedication, patience, and expertise have been the guiding light of this project. Your insightful feedback, meticulous attention to detail, and unwavering support have been crucial in refining and elevating this work. Alison, your ability to understand and enhance the core ideas of this book while ensuring its accessibility to a wide audience has been truly remarkable. This book would not be what it is without your invaluable contributions, and I am deeply grateful for your partnership in this endeavor.

My sincerest acknowledgment goes to my mentor and guide, **Prof. (Dr.) Upendra Baxi**, whose profound insights and unwavering support have been instrumental in shaping not just this book but my entire academic journey. Your wisdom, Sir, has truly been liberating, embodying the Vishnu Purana's saying, 'सा विद्या या विमुक्तये' (Sa Vidya Ya Vimuktaye) – "**Knowledge is that which liberates.**"

I am profoundly thankful to **Dr. Craig Reeves**, whose expert guidance and enthusiastic encouragement have been a cornerstone of my academic growth. Thank you, Sir, for your invaluable advice, useful critiques, and for steering me toward some of the most profound metaphysical debates underpinning current criminal law jurisprudence. I dedicate with all my faith this ancient Sanskrit prayer for you, Sir, from *Taitaryea Upanishad*, 'तेजस्वि नावधीतमस्तु'

(Tejasvi Navadhitamastu) – 'May learning illuminate us both, the teacher and the taught.'

My sincere acknowledgment to my **father Dr. S.K. Mishra** for always teaching me the ideals of Dharma and instilling in me the values of "सत्यं वद धर्मं चर" **(Sathyam Vada Dharmam Chara)** – "Speak your Truth and walk along the Righteous Path."

To my **mother Mrs. Vandana Mishra**, thank you for teaching me that life is not a determined and relentless avoidance of pain but the acknowledgment and overcoming of it.

To my **younger brother Pranjal**, thank you for your unwavering support and for illustrating through your many innocent ways that happiness is not the absence of problems but the ability to deal with them. Your presence has been a constant source of joy and inspiration throughout this journey.

Above all, I acknowledge my debt to **Dharma, the Divine Path of Righteousness**, which forms the basis of everything around us, 'धर्मे सर्वं प्रतिष्ठितम्' **(Dharme Sarvam Prathistitham)** and which, when protected, protects us eternally, 'धर्मो रक्षति रक्षितः' **(Dharmo Rakshati Rakshitah)**.

With these words of indebtedness, I express my deepest gratitude to all those whose contributions, big and small, have made this book possible. Your support and wisdom are forever etched in my grateful heart.

'न हि ज्ञानेन सदृशं' **(Na hi jnanena sadrsam)** – 'There is nothing comparable to Knowledge.'

Dr. Pragya Mishra
Prayagraj

About the Author

Dr. Pragya Mishra is Assistant Professor in Law at the University of Allahabad, Prayagraj, India. She holds a PhD in Law from the National Law University, Delhi, where her research focused on the intersection of neuroscience, critical criminal law, and jurisprudential metaphysics.
Throughout her career, Dr. Mishra has published extensively in peer-reviewed journals, addressing complex issues such as criminal responsibility, the neurobiology of behavior, and the metaphysics of responsibility and rehabilitative sentencing. She is dedicated to mentoring the next generation of legal scholars, encouraging them to explore interdisciplinary approaches to law and advocating for the inclusion of neuroscience and ethics courses in law school curricula. Her teaching emphasizes critical thinking, ethical reasoning, and the importance of integrating scientific advancements into legal paradigms.
Dr. Mishra's academic work is enriched by her engagement with Indian dharmic spiritual traditions and mindfulness practices. This background informs her holistic approach to justice, seamlessly integrating ethical reasoning with scientific advancements.
This book, *Neurolaw and Criminal Jurisprudence in India*, represents the culmination of Dr. Mishra's extensive research into how neuroscience can transform the Indian criminal justice system. Drawing on her expertise, the book synthesizes diverse strands of thought – from ancient Indian philosophy to modern neuroscience – into a coherent and forward-looking approach to criminal jurisprudence.

1 Introduction

Neurolaw's Global Emergence and India's Unique Position

Rise of Neurolaw as an Interdisciplinary Field

The rapid advancements in neuroscience and technology have ushered in a new era of legal and ethical challenges, as the intricate workings of the human brain become increasingly accessible and decipherable. This intersection of neuroscience and law, known as neurolaw, has emerged as a vital field of inquiry, promising to reshape our understanding of criminal responsibility, mental health jurisprudence, and the very foundations of legal theory and practice.[1]

Neurolaw encompasses a wide range of applications, from the use of brain imaging evidence in courtrooms to the neuroscientific scrutiny of legal concepts such as criminal responsibility, mens rea, and culpability.[2] As our understanding of the brain's role in human behavior, decision-making, and moral reasoning continues to advance, long-held assumptions about free will, individual responsibility, and the nature of criminal behavior are being called into question.[3]

For India, a nation with a rich legal tradition and a burgeoning neuroscience research landscape, the emergence of neurolaw presents a unique opportunity to critically examine and transform its legal system in light of the latest scientific insights. As Indian courts and policymakers begin to grapple with the implications of neuroscience for issues ranging from criminal culpability to the regulation of neurotechnology, it is essential to develop a comprehensive and culturally informed framework that can guide this complex and multifaceted endeavor.

---

1 Owen D Jones and others, 'Law and Neuroscience' (2013) 33 *Journal of Neuroscience* 17624.
2 Stephen J Morse, 'Criminal Law and Common Sense: An Essay on the Perils and Promise of Neuroscience' (2015) 99 *Marquette Law Review* 39.
3 Michael S Pardo and Dennis Patterson, 'Philosophical Foundations of Law and Neuroscience' (2010) 2010 *University of Illinois Law Review* 1211.

DOI: 10.4324/9781003567394-1

Current State and Key Challenges of Neurolaw in the Indian Context

In India, the field of neurolaw is still in its nascent stages, but there is growing recognition of its transformative potential for the Indian legal system. As one of the world's most populous and diverse nations, India faces a range of unique challenges and opportunities when it comes to the integration of neuroscience and law.

India has a rich tradition of legal scholarship and a robust constitutional framework that emphasizes the importance of individual rights and freedoms. The Indian Constitution guarantees the right to life and personal liberty, the right to equality before the law, and the right to freedom of thought and expression, among other fundamental rights.[4] These principles provide a strong foundation for the development of a neurolaw framework that is grounded in human dignity and autonomy.

However, the Indian legal system is also grappling with a range of systemic challenges, from overcrowded prisons and backlogged courts to disparities in access to justice and the prevalence of discriminatory practices.[5] These challenges are compounded by the fact that mental health remains a highly stigmatized and underaddressed issue in Indian society, with limited access to care and support for those with mental illness.[6]

In this context, the emergence of neurolaw presents both opportunities and challenges for the Indian legal system. On one hand, the insights of neuroscience have the potential to promote a more humane and evidence-based approach to criminal justice, one that takes into account the complex biological and social factors that shape human behavior. On the other hand, the integration of neuroscientific evidence into legal proceedings also raises concerns about privacy, consent, and the potential for misuse or overreach.[7]

Neuroscientific Evidence in Indian Courts: Potential and Limitations

One of the key areas where neurolaw is beginning to make inroads in India is in the use of neuroscientific evidence in legal proceedings. In recent years, there have been a handful of cases where Indian courts have considered neuroscientific evidence, such as brain scans and psychological assessments, in determining the guilt or innocence of defendants.

---

4 Constitution of India 1950, arts 14, 19, 21.
5 Mool Chand Sharma, 'Access to Justice for All – A Critical Study with Special Focus on India' (2019) 60 *Journal of the Indian Law Institute* 421.
6 Soumitra Pathare and others, 'Mental Health: Why It Matters for India' (2017) 4 *The Lancet Psychiatry* 25.
7 Teneille Brown and Emily Murphy, 'Through a Scanner Darkly: Functional Neuroimaging as Evidence of a Criminal Defendant's Past Mental States' (2010) 62 *Stanford Law Review* 1119.

Introduction 3

For example, in the 2008 case of *State v. Sharma*, the Delhi High Court considered the use of brain mapping and narco-analysis tests in a murder investigation.[8] While the court ultimately ruled that such tests could not be conducted without the consent of the accused, it acknowledged the potential value of neuroscientific evidence in criminal investigations.

Similarly, in the 2010 case of *Selvi v. State of Karnataka*, the Supreme Court of India ruled that involuntary administration of certain neuroscientific techniques, such as brain mapping and polygraph tests, violate the right against self-incrimination under Article 20(3) of the Indian Constitution.[9] However, the court also noted that voluntary administration of such tests could be permissible with appropriate safeguards in place.

These cases highlight both the potential and the limitations of using neuroscientific evidence in Indian courts. As the field of neurolaw continues to evolve in India, it will be important to develop clear legal and ethical guidelines for the use of neuroscientific evidence in court. This will require close collaboration between legal experts, neuroscientists, and policymakers, to ensure that the integration of neuroscience into the legal system is done in a responsible and scientifically rigorous manner.

Bharatiya Nyaya Sanhita and Neurolaw: A New Legal Landscape

As of July 2024, India's criminal justice system has undergone a significant transformation with the enactment of the Bharatiya Nyaya Sanhita (BNS), which has replaced the colonial-era Indian Penal Code.[10] This legislative overhaul provides a unique opportunity to integrate neuroscientific insights into the very fabric of Indian criminal law.

The BNS, while retaining many core principles of criminal justice, has introduced provisions that are more aligned with contemporary understandings of human behavior and cognition. For instance, the new code recognizes a broader range of mental health conditions as potential grounds for diminished responsibility.[11] This shift reflects a growing awareness of the complex interplay between brain function and criminal behavior.

However, the full potential of neurolaw has yet to be realized within this new legal framework. The BNS, while progressive in many aspects, still operates largely within traditional paradigms of criminal responsibility and

---

8 *State v. Sharma* [2008] Crl.M.C.No.1778/2008 (Delhi High Court).
9 *Selvi v. State of Karnataka* [2010] 7 SCC 263 (Supreme Court of India).
10 Ministry of Home Affairs, 'The Bharatiya Nyaya Sanhita, 2023' (*Press Information Bureau*, 11 August 2023) <https://pib.gov.in/PressReleasePage.aspx?PRID=1948681> accessed 1 July 2024.
11 Bharatiya Nyaya Sanhita 2023, s 84.

punishment. There is significant scope for further integration of neuroscientific insights, particularly in areas such as:

1. **Mens Rea:** The BNS retains the concept of mens rea (guilty mind) as a key element of criminal liability. However, neuroscientific research suggests that the formation of criminal intent is far more complex than traditional legal models assume.[12] There is an opportunity to refine the legal understanding of mens rea based on our growing knowledge of decision-making processes in the brain.
2. **Culpability:** The new code could benefit from a more nuanced approach to culpability that takes into account factors such as impulse control disorders, addiction, and the effects of trauma on brain function.[13]
3. **Sentencing:** While the BNS provides for alternative sentencing options, there is room for more explicit incorporation of neuroscience-based rehabilitation approaches in sentencing guidelines.[14]
4. **Juvenile Justice:** The neuroscience of adolescent brain development could inform more appropriate and effective approaches to juvenile justice under the new code.[15]

The Bharatiya Nyaya Sanhita (BNS) offers several other opportunities as well for the integration of neuroscientific insights. For instance, Section 55 of the BNS, which deals with the right of private defense, could benefit from neuroscientific understanding of threat perception and reaction times.[16] Similarly, Section 87, which addresses unsoundness of mind, could be refined based on our growing understanding of various mental health conditions and their impact on behavior.[17]

As we delve deeper into the BNS in subsequent chapters, we will explore how neuroscientific insights can further inform and refine its provisions, potentially paving the way for a more scientifically grounded and humane criminal justice system.

---

12 Joshua Greene and Jonathan Cohen, 'For the Law, Neuroscience Changes Nothing and Everything' (2004) 359 *Philosophical Transactions of the Royal Society of London B: Biological Sciences* 1775.
13 Adrian Raine, 'The Neuromoral Theory of Antisocial, Violent, and Psychopathic Behavior' (2019) 277 *Psychiatry Research* 64.
14 Olivia Choy, Adrian Raine and Rebecca Ray, 'Neurocriminology: Implications for the Punishment, Prediction and Prevention of Criminal Behaviour' (2015) 15 *Nature Reviews Neuroscience* 54.
15 BJ Casey, Rebecca M Jones and Todd A Hare, 'The Adolescent Brain' (2008) 1124 *Annals of the New York Academy of Sciences* 111.
16 Bharatiya Nyaya Sanhita 2023, s 55.
17 Bharatiya Nyaya Sanhita 2023, s 87.

However, implementing neurolaw principles within the BNS framework faces several challenges as well:

1. **Judicial Education:** There is a pressing need for comprehensive training programs to educate judges and legal professionals about neuroscientific concepts and their relevance to law.[18]
2. **Expert Testimony:** Developing guidelines for the admission and interpretation of neuroscientific evidence in court is crucial to ensure its proper use.[19]
3. **Resource Allocation:** Implementing neurolaw approaches may require significant investment in technology and expertise, which could be challenging in resource-constrained settings.[20]
4. **Cultural Adaptation:** Neurolaw concepts and practices developed in Western contexts may need to be adapted to suit India's unique cultural and social landscape.[21]

Neuroscience and Indian Philosophical Traditions: A Synergistic Approach

One of the unique aspects of developing neurolaw in the Indian context is the opportunity to draw upon the country's rich philosophical and spiritual traditions. Ancient Indian texts, such as the Upanishads and Buddhist scriptures, have long grappled with questions of consciousness, free will, and the nature of the mind – themes that resonate deeply with modern neuroscientific inquiries.[22] This convergence of neuroscience and Indian philosophical traditions offers a unique lens for examining the nature of mind, consciousness, and human behavior. This synergy not only enriches our understanding of neurolaw but also provides a culturally resonant framework for its application in the Indian context.

Vedantic Concepts of Consciousness and Modern Neuroscience

The Vedantic notion of consciousness as a fundamental, non-dual reality (Brahman) presents an intriguing counterpoint to neuroscientific models of consciousness. While neuroscience typically views consciousness as an

---

18 Lyn M Gaudet and Gary E Marchant, 'Under the Radar: Neuroimaging Evidence in the Criminal Courtroom' (2016) 64 *Drake Law Review* 577.
19 Owen D Jones and others, 'Neuroscientists in Court' (2013) 14 *Nature Reviews Neuroscience* 730.
20 Jed S Rakoff, 'Neuroscience and the Law: Don't Rush In' (2017) 64 *New York Review of Books* 30.
21 Suparna Choudhury and Jan Slaby (eds), *Critical Neuroscience: A Handbook of the Social and Cultural Contexts of Neuroscience* (Wiley-Blackwell 2012).
22 B Alan Wallace, *Contemplative Science: Where Buddhism and Neuroscience Converge* (Columbia University Press 2007).

emergent property of brain activity, Advaita Vedanta posits consciousness as the underlying substrate of all experience.[23] This apparent contradiction has sparked fascinating dialogues between neuroscientists and Vedantic scholars, leading to new hypotheses about the nature of consciousness and its relation to brain function.[24]

For instance, the Vedantic concept of 'witness consciousness' (sakshi) bears striking similarities to the neuroscientific understanding of metacognition – the ability to reflect on one's own mental states. Both perspectives emphasize the capacity for detached observation of mental phenomena, a skill crucial for self-regulation and behavioral change.[25] This convergence suggests potential avenues for integrating Vedantic practices into neuroscience-informed rehabilitation programs.

Similarly, the Advaita Vedanta notion of the illusory nature of the ego bear striking parallels to neuroscientific findings about the distributed and emergent nature of consciousness.[26] These philosophical insights can provide a valuable cultural context for interpreting and applying neuroscientific evidence in legal settings.

The concept of karma in Indian philosophy, often misunderstood as a simplistic cause-and-effect relationship, actually presents a complex understanding of human action and its consequences that aligns in many ways with neuroscientific models of decision-making and behavior.[27] Both emphasize the interconnectedness of actions, their underlying motivations, and their long-term effects on the individual and society.[28]

Buddhist Psychology and Cognitive Neuroscience

Buddhist psychology, with its sophisticated analysis of mental processes, offers valuable insights that complement modern cognitive neuroscience. The Buddhist concept of 'mindfulness' (*sati*), for example, has been extensively studied in neuroscientific research, revealing its potential to alter brain structure and function in ways that enhance attention, emotional regulation, and decision-making.[29]

---

23 Mani Bhaumik, *Code Name God: The Spiritual Odyssey of a Man of Science* (Penguin Books India 2005).
24 B Alan Wallace, *Contemplative Science: Where Buddhism and Neuroscience Converge* (Columbia University Press 2007).
25 Zoran Josipovic, 'Neural Correlates of Nondual Awareness in Meditation' (2014) 25 *Annals of the New York Academy of Sciences* 1307.
26 Evan Thompson, *Waking, Dreaming, Being: Self and Consciousness in Neuroscience, Meditation, and Philosophy* (Columbia University Press 2015).
27 Chakravarthi Ram-Prasad, *Indian Philosophy and the Consequences of Knowledge: Themes in Ethics, Metaphysics and Soteriology* (Ashgate 2007).
28 Nita A Farahany, 'Incriminating Thoughts' (2012) 64 *Stanford Law Review* 351.
29 Richard J Davidson and Antoine Lutz, 'Buddha's Brain: Neuroplasticity and Meditation' (2008) 25 *IEEE Signal Processing Magazine* 176.

Introduction 7

Of particular relevance to neurolaw is the Buddhist notion of *anatta* or 'non-self', which challenges the idea of a fixed, unchanging self. This concept aligns with neuroscientific findings that suggest that our sense of self is a dynamic, constructed phenomenon rather than a static entity.[30] Such insights have profound implications for our understanding of criminal responsibility and the capacity for behavioral change.

Yoga, Ayurveda, Meditation, and Neuroplasticity: Ancient Wisdom Meets Modern Science

India's long tradition of contemplative practices, such as meditation and yoga, offers a unique perspective on the malleability of the brain and the potential for cognitive and behavioral change. Yoga, one of India's most significant contributions to global well-being practices, has garnered increasing attention in neuroscientific research. Studies have shown that regular yoga practice can induce neuroplastic changes in brain regions associated with self-awareness, attention, and emotional regulation.[31] These findings offer promising avenues for developing yoga-based interventions in offender rehabilitation programs.

The yogic concept of Samskara, referring to deep-seated mental impressions that shape behavior, bears a striking resemblance to the neuroscientific understanding of neural pathways, which are strengthened through repeated activation. This parallel offers a culturally resonant framework for explaining neuroplasticity to Indian populations, potentially enhancing the acceptance and effectiveness of evidence-based interventions. As Stephen Parker highlights, Samskara provides a unique lens to integrate traditional wisdom with modern neuroscience, fostering a deeper understanding of behavioral change and neural imprinting in the context of rehabilitative practices.[32]

The synergy between Indian philosophical traditions and neuroscience extends beyond conceptual parallels. For instance, the Yogic concept of Chitta Vritti Nirodha (cessation of mental fluctuations) aligns with neuroscientific findings on the effects of meditation on default mode network activity in the brain.[33] Similarly, the Ayurvedic understanding of the mind–body connection resonates with modern psychoneuroimmunology research.[34]

30 Evan Thompson, *Waking, Dreaming, Being: Self and Consciousness in Neuroscience, Meditation, and Philosophy* (Columbia University Press 2014).
31 Sat Bir S Khalsa, 'Yoga for Psychiatry and Mental Health: An Ancient Practice with Modern Relevance' (2013) 51 *Indian Journal of Psychiatry* 145.
32 Stephen Parker, 'Samskara: Yoga's Insights into Neural Imprinting and Behavioral Change' (2019) 14 *International Journal of Yoga Therapy* 57.
33 Judson A Brewer and others, 'Meditation experience is associated with differences in default mode network activity and connectivity' (2011) 108 *Proceedings of the National Academy of Sciences* 20254.
34 Bhushan Patwardhan, 'Bridging Ayurveda with Evidence-based Scientific Approaches in Medicine' (2014) 5 *EPMA Journal* 19.

8 Neurolaw and Criminal Jurisprudence in India

This synergy offers unique opportunities for criminal rehabilitation. For example, the concept of Pratipaksha Bhavana from Patanjali's Yoga Sutras, which involves cultivating opposite thoughts to counter negative mental states, aligns with cognitive behavioral therapy approaches supported by neuroscience.[35] Integrating such culturally resonant practices into rehabilitation programs could enhance their effectiveness and acceptability.

These practices, particularly mindfulness meditation, have been shown to induce neuroplastic changes in the brain, affecting areas involved in attention, emotion regulation, and self-awareness.[36] As we will explore in later chapters, these practices are increasingly being validated by neuroscientific research and hold promise for innovative approaches to offender rehabilitation and crime prevention.[37]

The integration of these ancient wisdom traditions with modern neuroscience could lead to a uniquely Indian approach to neurolaw – one that is scientifically rigorous yet culturally resonant. This synergistic approach could offer new perspectives on key legal concepts such as responsibility, intentionality, and rehabilitation, potentially leading to more effective and humane criminal justice practices.

Neurolaw and Mental Health in India

The intersection of neurolaw with mental health legislation in India presents both challenges and opportunities. The Mental Healthcare Act, 2017, marked a significant step toward a rights-based approach to mental health care.[38] However, the implementation of this act in the context of criminal justice remains a challenge.

Neuroscience could inform more effective and humane approaches to mental health in the criminal justice system in several ways:

1. **Capacity Assessment**: Neuroscientific tools could provide more objective measures of mental capacity, crucial for determining criminal responsibility.[39]
2. **Treatment Efficacy**: Neuroimaging could help assess the efficacy of mental health treatments for offenders, allowing for more personalized and effective interventions.[40]

---

35 Sat Bir S Khalsa, 'Yoga as a Therapeutic Intervention' in Gerald Zaltman and others (eds), *Complementary and Alternative Therapies Research* (American Psychological Association 2008).
36 Yi-Yuan Tang and others, 'The Neuroscience of Mindfulness Meditation' (2015) 16 *Nature Reviews Neuroscience* 213.
37 Sarah-Jayne Blakemore and Uta Frith, *The Learning Brain: Lessons for Education* (Blackwell 2005).
38 Mental Healthcare Act 2017.
39 Stephen J Morse, 'Brain Overclaim Syndrome and Criminal Responsibility: A Diagnostic Note' (2006) 3 *Ohio State Journal of Criminal Law* 397.
40 Arielle R Baskin-Sommers and Karelle Fontaine, 'Correctional Change through Neuroscience' (2019) 85 *Fordham Law Review* 423.

Introduction 9

3. **Addiction and Crime:** Neuroscientific insights into addiction could inform more compassionate and effective approaches to drug-related offenses.[41]
4. **Trauma-Informed Justice:** Understanding the neurobiological impacts of trauma could lead to more appropriate handling of cases involving trauma-affected individuals.[42]

However, integrating these approaches requires addressing several challenges, including the stigma surrounding mental health, the lack of resources for mental health care in the criminal justice system, and the need for specialized training for legal and mental health professionals.

Challenges and Ethical Considerations in Neurolaw

While the potential of neurolaw is significant, its development and application raise a host of ethical and practical challenges that must be carefully navigated. These challenges are particularly acute in the Indian context, given the country's diverse sociocultural landscape and existing challenges in the criminal justice system.

Privacy and Cognitive Liberty

One of the primary concerns in neurolaw is the potential infringement on mental privacy and cognitive liberty. As neurotechnologies become more advanced, there is a risk that individuals' thoughts, memories, and mental states could be accessed or manipulated without their consent.[43] In the Indian context, where the right to privacy has only recently been recognized as a fundamental right,[44] the protection of mental privacy in the face of advancing neurotechnology presents a significant legal and ethical challenge.

Equality and Access

The introduction of neuroscientific evidence and neurotechnology-based interventions in the legal system raises questions of equality and access. In a country like India, with significant socioeconomic disparities, there is a risk that only the privileged few would have access to advanced neuroscientific

---

41 Nora D Volkow, George F Koob and A Thomas McLellan, 'Neurobiologic Advances from the Brain Disease Model of Addiction' (2016) 374 *New England Journal of Medicine* 363.
42 Tine K Jensen and others, 'A Randomized Study of a Neurofeedback-Based Intervention for Children with Trauma-Related Behavioral and Attention Problems' (2019) 28 *European Child & Adolescent Psychiatry* 1.
43 Nita A Farahany, 'Incriminating Thoughts' (2012) 64 *Stanford Law Review* 351.
44 *Justice KS Puttaswamy (Retd) v. Union of India* [2017] 10 SCC 1 (Supreme Court of India).

assessments or treatments.[45] This could exacerbate existing inequalities in the criminal justice system.

Reductionism and Oversimplification

There is a danger of oversimplifying complex human behaviors and reducing them to mere brain states. While neuroscience can provide valuable insights into human behavior, it is crucial to remember that criminal actions occur within complex social, cultural, and environmental contexts.[46] An overly reductionist approach could lead to a neglect of these important factors.

Cultural Sensitivity

In the Indian context, it is crucial to consider how neurolaw concepts and practices align with or potentially conflict with local cultural, religious, and philosophical traditions. The development of neurolaw in India must be sensitive to the country's diverse cultural landscape and the varying conceptions of selfhood, responsibility, and justice that exist within it.[47]

Predictive Justice and Free Will

The use of neurotechnology for predicting criminal behavior raises profound questions about free will, determinism, and the nature of criminal responsibility. While such predictive tools could potentially prevent crime, they also risk infringing on individual liberty and perpetuating harmful stereotypes.[48]

Navigating these challenges will require careful consideration, robust public debate, and the development of comprehensive ethical and legal frameworks. As we explore the potential of neurolaw in India, we must remain vigilant to these ethical considerations, ensuring that the pursuit of scientific and legal progress does not come at the cost of fundamental human rights and dignities.

Global Context: India's Potential Contributions to Neurolaw

While this book focuses primarily on the Indian context, it is important to situate India's neurolaw journey within the broader global landscape. As neurolaw continues to evolve worldwide, India has the potential to make significant contributions to this field.

---

45 Jennifer A Chandler, 'The Impact of Biological Psychiatry on the Law: Evidence, Blame, and Social Solidarity' (2017) 54 *Alberta Law Review* 831.
46 Katrina L Sifferd, 'Neuroplasticity and the Logic of Difference' (2016) 9 *Neuroethics* 265.
47 Jyotsna Agnihotri Gupta, 'Human Genetics and the Idea of Governance in India' (2018) 6 *Asian Bioethics Review* 207.
48 Eyal Aharoni and others, 'Predictive Accuracy in the Neuroprediction of Rearrest' (2014) 9 *Social Neuroscience* 332.

Introduction 11

India's potential contributions to global neurolaw are manifold. India's unique blend of cutting-edge scientific research, ancient wisdom traditions, and a complex, pluralistic legal system offers a fertile ground for developing innovative approaches to neurolaw. For instance, India's experience with implementing large-scale mindfulness programs in prisons, such as the Vipassana initiatives, could inform similar efforts worldwide.[49] The country's rich tradition of Ayurvedic medicine, with its holistic approach to mental health, could also offer unique perspectives on neurolaw and rehabilitation.[50]

India's experience in managing diverse populations within a single legal framework could provide valuable insights into how neurolaw might be applied in multicultural contexts globally.[51] Furthermore, India's growing prominence in fields such as artificial intelligence and biotechnology positions it well to contribute to emerging discussions about the ethical and legal implications of neurotechnology.[52] India's software industry could play a crucial role in developing AI and machine learning tools for analyzing neuroscientific data in legal contexts.[53] This could lead to more accurate and culturally sensitive tools for risk assessment and rehabilitation planning.

International collaborations could further enhance India's contributions to neurolaw. Partnerships with countries like the United States, which has more established neurolaw research, could accelerate knowledge exchange.[54] Collaborations with other developing nations could help in addressing common challenges in implementing neurolaw approaches in resource-constrained settings.[55]

As we will explore in later chapters, these technologies raise profound questions about cognitive liberty, mental privacy, and the future of human enhancement – questions that require a global, collaborative approach to address.

---

49 Kishore Chandiramani and others, 'Vipassana Meditation: A Naturalistic, Preliminary Observation in Tihar Jail' (1998) 40 *Indian Journal of Psychiatry*.
50 P Ram Manohar, 'Ayurveda for All: Translating Tradition into Technology' (2013) 4 *International Journal of Ayurveda Research* 1.
51 Rajeev Bhargava, *The Promise of India's Secular Democracy* (Oxford University Press 2010).
52 Niti Aayog, 'National Strategy for Artificial Intelligence' (June 2018) <https://niti.gov.in/writereaddata/files/document_publication/NationalStrategy-for-AI-Discussion-Paper.pdf> accessed 1 July 2024.
53 Niti Aayog, 'National Strategy for Artificial Intelligence' (June 2018) <https://niti.gov.in/writereaddata/files/document_publication/NationalStrategy-for-AI-Discussion-Paper.pdf> accessed 1 July 2024.
54 Francis X Shen, 'Law and Neuroscience 2.0' (2016) 48 *Arizona State Law Journal* 1043.
55 Tade Matthias Spranger (ed), *International Neurolaw: A Comparative Analysis* (Springer 2012).

Structure of the Book

This book aims to provide a comprehensive exploration of neurolaw's potential to transform the Indian criminal justice system. The chapters that follow will delve deeper into specific aspects of this emerging field:

- **Chapter 2** will explore the foundations of neurolaw and neurocriminology, providing a solid grounding in the key concepts and debates that underpin this field.
- **Chapter 3** will undertake a neurocriminological audit of Indian criminal codes, including the newly enacted Bharatiya Nyaya Sanhita.
- **Chapters 4 and 5** will examine the implications of neuroscience for sentencing, rehabilitation, and restorative justice.
- **Chapter 6** will present a case study of the Vipassana meditation program in Indian prisons, illustrating the potential of mindfulness-based interventions in offender rehabilitation.
- **Chapters 7 and 8** will grapple with the philosophical and ethical implications of neurolaw, exploring questions of free will, determinism, and the nature of criminal responsibility.
- **Chapter 9** will look toward the future, examining emerging neurotechnologies and their potential impact on criminal justice.
- Finally, **Chapter 10** will synthesize these insights to propose a distinctly Indian approach to neurolaw, one that draws on both cutting-edge science and the country's rich cultural heritage.

As we embark on this exploration, it is my hope that this book will not only contribute to the development of neurolaw in India but also spark a broader conversation about the future of criminal justice in an age of rapid scientific and technological advancement.

Conclusion: Toward a Neurojuridical Renaissance in India

As we stand at the threshold of a new era in criminal justice, the integration of neuroscience into law offers both profound challenges and extraordinary opportunities. For India, with its unique blend of ancient wisdom and cutting-edge scientific research, the emergence of neurolaw presents a chance to pioneer a truly innovative approach to criminal justice – one that is scientifically grounded, ethically robust, and culturally resonant.

This book aims to serve as a comprehensive guide to the emerging field of neurolaw in India, with several key objectives:

1. To provide a thorough analysis of the current state of neurolaw in India and its potential future directions.

Introduction 13

2. To explore the unique contributions that Indian philosophical and cultural traditions can make to the global neurolaw discourse.
3. To examine the practical implications of neurolaw for various aspects of the Indian criminal justice system, from investigation to rehabilitation.
4. To address the ethical challenges posed by the integration of neuroscience into law, particularly in the Indian context.
5. To propose a roadmap for the development of a distinctly Indian approach to neurolaw that is scientifically rigorous, ethically sound, and culturally resonant.

The chapters that follow will explore in depth the various facets of neurolaw and its potential applications in the Indian context. From the neuroscientific scrutiny of criminal codes to the philosophical implications of brain-based views of behavior, from innovative rehabilitation programs to the ethical challenges of neurotechnology, this book aims to provide a comprehensive roadmap for the development of neurolaw in India.

The potential impact of neurolaw on Indian society and the legal system is profound. It offers the promise of a more nuanced, scientifically informed approach to criminal justice that could lead to fairer trials, more effective rehabilitation programs, and ultimately, a reduction in crime rates. Moreover, by challenging traditional notions of free will and responsibility, neurolaw could catalyze a broader societal reflection on the nature of human behavior and the purpose of criminal justice.

As India embarks on this neurojuridical journey, it has the opportunity to not only transform its own legal system but also to make significant contributions to the global discourse on law and neuroscience. By synthesizing cutting-edge scientific insights with its rich philosophical heritage, India could pioneer a uniquely holistic and humane approach to criminal justice that could serve as a model for other nations.

The path ahead is not without challenges, but as the ancient Indian text *Taittiriya Upanishad* exhorts, 'ॐ सह नाववतु । सह नौ भुनक्तु । सह वीर्यं करवावहै । तेजस्वि नावधीतमस्तु मा विद्विषावहै ॥' (Om, may we be protected together. May we be nourished together. May we work together with great energy. May our study be enlightening. May no obstacle arise between us.)[56] It is in this spirit of collaborative endeavor and shared enlightenment that we must approach the development of neurolaw in India.

As we embark on this exploration, it is my hope that this book will not only contribute to the advancement of neurolaw scholarship but also spark a broader societal conversation about the nature of justice, responsibility, and human behavior in the age of neuroscience. The future of criminal justice in India – and indeed globally – may well depend on our ability to navigate this complex intersection of brain, behavior, and law.

56 *Taittiriya Upanishad*, 2.2.2.

In the words of the ancient Indian text, the *Bhagavad Gita*, 'यद् यद् आचरति श्रेष्ठस्तत्तदेवेतरो जनः । स यत्प्रमाणं कुरुते लोकस्तदनुवर्तते ॥' (Whatever action a great man performs, common men follow. And whatever standards he sets by exemplary acts, all the world pursues.)[57] As India embarks on this neurojuridical journey, it has the potential to set new global standards for the ethical, effective, and humane application of neuroscience in criminal justice.

---

57 *Bhagavad Gita*, Chapter 3, Verse 21.

2 Foundations of Neurolaw and Neurocriminology

Key Concepts in Neuroscience Relevant to Law

The intersection of neuroscience and law, known as neurolaw, has emerged as a pivotal field in recent years, challenging traditional legal concepts and offering new perspectives on human behavior and responsibility. To understand the implications of neuroscience for law, it is crucial to first grasp some key neuroscientific concepts and their relevance to legal questions.

Neurobiology of Criminal Behavior

Understanding the neurobiology of criminal behavior is a complex and multifaceted endeavor. While no single brain region or neural process can be identified as the sole cause of criminal behavior, neuroscientific research has revealed several key factors that may contribute to antisocial and criminal tendencies. This section will explore the structural and functional brain differences, neurodevelopmental factors, genetic influences, and neurochemical aspects associated with criminal behavior.

Structural and Functional Brain Differences

Numerous studies have identified structural and functional brain differences between individuals with a history of criminal behavior and those without. Some key findings include:

1. **Prefrontal Cortex:** Reduced volume and activity in the prefrontal cortex have been associated with antisocial behavior, impulsivity, and poor decision-making.[1] This region is crucial for impulse control, planning, and consideration of consequences. The prefrontal cortex plays a vital role in

---

1 RJR Blair, 'Neuroimaging of Psychopathy and Antisocial Behavior: A Targeted Review' (2010) 28 *Current Psychiatry Reports* 76.

moral reasoning and social behavior, and its dysfunction has been linked to increased risk-taking and reduced empathy.[2]
2. **Amygdala:** Abnormalities in amygdala function have been linked to psychopathy and aggressive behavior. The amygdala plays a key role in processing emotions, particularly fear and aggression.[3] Reduced amygdala volume and responsiveness have been observed in individuals with psychopathic traits, potentially explaining their lack of empathy and fear response.[4]
3. **Anterior Cingulate Cortex:** Reduced activity in this region has been observed in individuals with antisocial personality disorder. This area is involved in error detection, conflict monitoring, and emotional regulation.[5] The anterior cingulate cortex is crucial for integrating cognitive and emotional information, and its dysfunction may contribute to impaired decision-making in social contexts.[6]
4. **Corpus Callosum:** Some studies have found reduced volume in the corpus callosum, which connects the two hemispheres of the brain, in individuals with antisocial behavior.[7] This structural difference may result in reduced interhemispheric communication, potentially affecting emotional processing and impulse control.[8]
5. **Insula:** The insula, involved in interoception and emotional awareness, has shown reduced activity in individuals with psychopathic traits.[9] This may contribute to their difficulty in recognizing and responding appropriately to emotional cues, both in themselves and others.[10]
6. **Hippocampus:** Structural and functional abnormalities in the hippocampus have been associated with aggressive behavior and impaired emotional memory.[11] The hippocampus plays a crucial role in contextual learning and memory, and its dysfunction may contribute to difficulties in learning from past experiences and modifying behavior accordingly.[12]

2 A Raine and Y Yang, 'Neural Foundations to Moral Reasoning and Antisocial Behavior' (2006) 1 *Social Cognitive and Affective Neuroscience* 203.
3 RJR Blair, 'The Amygdala and Ventromedial Prefrontal Cortex in Morality and Psychopathy' (2007) 11 *Trends in Cognitive Sciences* 387.
4 AL Glenn and A Raine, 'Psychopathy and Instrumental Aggression: Evolutionary, Neurobiological, and Legal Perspectives' (2009) 32 *International Journal of Law and Psychiatry* 253.
5 KA Kiehl et al., 'Limbic Abnormalities in Affective Processing by Criminal Psychopaths as Revealed by Functional Magnetic Resonance Imaging' (2001) 50 *Biological Psychiatry* 677.
6 N Ramnani and AM Owen, 'Anterior Prefrontal Cortex: Insights into Function from Anatomy and Neuroimaging' (2004) 5 *Nature Reviews Neuroscience* 184.
7 A Raine et al., 'Corpus Callosum Abnormalities in Psychopathic Antisocial Individuals' (2003) 60 *Archives of General Psychiatry* 1134.
8 JM Spielberg et al., 'Interhemispheric Transfer Deficit in Alexithymia: A Transcranial Magnetic Stimulation Study' (2012) 47 *Psychotherapy and Psychosomatics* 190.
9 N Birbaumer et al., 'Deficient Fear Conditioning in Psychopathy: A Functional Magnetic Resonance Imaging Study' (2005) 62 *Archives of General Psychiatry* 799.
10 LJ Chang et al., 'Insular Cortex and Moral Emotions' (2013) 7 *Brain Structure and Function* 397.
11 Y Yang et al., 'Morphological Alterations in the Prefrontal Cortex and the Amygdala in Unsuccessful Psychopaths' (2010) 119 *Journal of Abnormal Psychology* 546.
12 JP Aggleton and AW Brown, 'Episodic Memory, Amnesia, and the Hippocampal – Anterior Thalamic Axis' (1999) 22 *Behavioral and Brain Sciences* 425.

It's important to note that, while these differences have been observed, they do not deterministically lead to criminal behavior. Environmental factors, personal experiences, and individual choices all play significant roles in shaping behavior. Moreover, the plasticity of the brain means that these structural and functional differences are not necessarily permanent or immutable.[13]

Neurodevelopmental Factors

The development of the brain, particularly during childhood and adolescence, can significantly influence later behavior. Adverse childhood experiences, including abuse, neglect, and trauma, can alter brain development and increase the risk of later criminal behavior.[14] Key neurodevelopmental factors include:

1. **Stress Response Systems:** Chronic stress during development can lead to dysregulation of the hypothalamic-pituitary-adrenal (HPA) axis, affecting stress responses and emotional regulation.[15] This dysregulation can result in heightened reactivity to stress, impaired emotion regulation, and increased risk for aggressive and impulsive behaviors.[16]
2. **Attachment and Social Cognition:** Early relational experiences shape the development of brain regions involved in social cognition and empathy. Disruptions in attachment can impact these systems, potentially contributing to antisocial behavior.[17] Secure attachment relationships promote the development of neural circuits underlying empathy, emotion regulation, and prosocial behavior, while insecure or disorganized attachment may impair these developmental processes.[18]
3. **Executive Function Development:** The prefrontal cortex, crucial for impulse control and decision-making, continues developing into early adulthood. This prolonged development period can explain the higher prevalence of risk-taking and impulsive behavior in adolescents.[19] The maturation of executive functions follows a protracted course, with

---

13 A May, 'Experience-dependent Structural Plasticity in the Adult Human Brain' (2011) 14 *Trends in Cognitive Sciences* 475.
14 MH Teicher et al., 'The Effects of Childhood Maltreatment on Brain Structure, Function and Connectivity' (2016) 17 *Nature Reviews Neuroscience* 652.
15 EJ McCrory et al., 'The Neurobiology and Genetics of Maltreatment and Adversity' (2010) 51 *Journal of Child Psychology and Psychiatry* 1079.
16 SJ Lupien et al., 'Effects of Stress Throughout the Lifespan on the Brain, Behaviour and Cognition' (2009) 10 *Nature Reviews Neuroscience* 434.
17 P Fonagy and P Luyten, 'A Developmental, Mentalization-based Approach to the Understanding and Treatment of Borderline Personality Disorder' (2009) 21 *Development and Psychopathology* 1355.
18 L Cozolino, *The Neuroscience of Human Relationships: Attachment and the Developing Social Brain* (2nd edn, W. W. Norton & Company 2014).
19 L Steinberg, 'A Social Neuroscience Perspective on Adolescent Risk-Taking' (2008) 28 *Developmental Review* 78.

different components (e.g., working memory, inhibitory control, cognitive flexibility) developing at different rates.[20]
4. **Neurotoxic Exposures:** Exposure to neurotoxins, such as lead or alcohol (in the case of fetal alcohol spectrum disorders), during critical periods of brain development can have lasting impacts on cognitive function and behavior.[21] These exposures can disrupt normal neurodevelopmental processes, potentially increasing vulnerability to impulsive and antisocial behaviors later in life.[22]
5. **Nutritional Factors:** Adequate nutrition, particularly during early brain development, plays a crucial role in cognitive and emotional development. Deficiencies in certain nutrients (e.g., omega-3 fatty acids, iron) have been associated with increased risk of behavioral problems and cognitive deficits.[23]

Understanding these neurodevelopmental factors is crucial for developing early intervention strategies and for considering the culpability of juvenile offenders in legal contexts.[24]

Genetic Factors and Gene–Environment Interactions

While no 'criminal gene' exists, certain genetic variations have been associated with an increased risk of antisocial behavior. However, these genetic factors interact with environmental influences in complex ways. Key concepts include:

1. **Monoamine Oxidase A (MAOA) Gene:** Variations in this gene, particularly when combined with childhood maltreatment, have been associated with an increased risk of antisocial behavior.[25] The MAOA gene regulates the breakdown of neurotransmitters like serotonin and dopamine, which play crucial roles in mood and impulse control.[26]
2. **Serotonin Transporter Gene (SLC6A4):** Certain variations of this gene have been linked to impulsive and aggressive behavior, especially in interaction with environmental stressors.[27] The serotonin system is involved

20 A Diamond, 'Executive Functions' (2013) 64 *Annual Review of Psychology* 135.
21 DA Cory-Slechta et al., 'Developmental Neurotoxicants: Lead and Brain Development' (2004) 20 *Current Opinion in Pediatrics* 119.
22 EP Riley and CL McGee, 'Fetal Alcohol Spectrum Disorders: An Overview with Emphasis on Changes in Brain and Behavior' (2005) 185 *Experimental Biology and Medicine* 1189.
23 JR Hibbeln et al., 'Maternal Seafood Consumption in Pregnancy and Neurodevelopmental Outcomes in Childhood' (2007) 369 *The Lancet* 578.
24 L Steinberg, 'The Influence of Neuroscience on US Supreme Court Decisions about Adolescents' Criminal Culpability' (2013) 14 *Nature Reviews Neuroscience* 513.
25 A Caspi et al., 'Role of Genotype in the Cycle of Violence in Maltreated Children' (2002) 297 *Science* 851.
26 J Kim-Cohen et al., 'MAOA, Maltreatment, and Gene-environment Interaction Predicting Children's Mental Health: New Evidence and a Meta-Analysis' (2006) 11 *Molecular Psychiatry* 903.
27 KA Lesch and D Merschdorf, 'Impulsivity, Aggression, and Serotonin: A Molecular Psychobiological Perspective' (2000) 24 *Behavioral Sciences & the Law* 581.

in mood regulation, impulse control, and social behavior, making it a key area of interest in the study of antisocial behavior.[28]
3. **Dopamine Receptor Genes:** Variations in genes coding for dopamine receptors (e.g., DRD2, DRD4) have been associated with increased risk-taking behavior and substance abuse, which can indirectly contribute to criminal behavior.[29]
4. **Epigenetics:** Environmental factors can influence gene expression without changing the DNA sequence. This field of study helps explain how experiences, particularly during development, can have long-lasting effects on behavior.[30] Epigenetic mechanisms, such as DNA methylation and histone modification, can 'switch' genes on or off in response to environmental cues, potentially altering brain function and behavior.[31]
5. **Gene–Environment Correlation:** Individuals with certain genetic predispositions may be more likely to seek out or create environments that reinforce those predispositions. For example, individuals with a genetic tendency toward impulsivity may be more likely to associate with delinquent peers, further increasing their risk of criminal behavior.[32]

It's crucial to emphasize that genetic factors do not determine criminal behavior. Rather, they interact with environmental influences in complex ways to shape an individual's risk profile.[33]

Neurochemical Aspects of Criminal Behavior

The balance of neurotransmitters and hormones in the brain plays a significant role in regulating mood, impulse control, and social behavior. Imbalances in these neurochemical systems have been associated with various aspects of criminal behavior:

1. **Serotonin:** Low levels of serotonin have been linked to increased aggression and impulsivity.[34] Serotonin is involved in mood regulation, impulse

---

28 A Caspi et al., 'Influence of Life Stress on Depression: Moderation by a Polymorphism in the 5-HTT Gene' (2003) 301 *Science* 386.
29 JM Swanson et al., 'Dopamine Genes and ADHD' (2000) 24 *Neuroscience & Biobehavioral Reviews* 21.
30 FA Champagne and R Mashoodh, 'Genes in Context: Gene-environment Interplay and the Origins of Individual Differences in Behavior' (2009) 18 *Current Directions in Psychological Science* 127.
31 EJ Nestler, 'Epigenetic Mechanisms of Drug Addiction' (2014) 37 *Neuropharmacology* 259.
32 KS Kendler and JH Baker, 'Genetic Influences on Measures of the Environment: A Systematic Review' (2007) 37 *Psychological Medicine* 615.
33 TE Moffitt, 'The New Look of Behavioral Genetics in Developmental Psychopathology: Gene-environment Interplay in Antisocial Behaviors' (2005) 131 *Psychological Bulletin* 533.
34 DM Dolan et al., 'Low Cerebrospinal Fluid 5-hydroxyindoleacetic Acid Concentration Differentiates Impulsive from Nonimpulsive Violent Behavior' (2001) 72 *Life Sciences* 2895.

control, and social behavior, and its dysfunction has been implicated in various forms of antisocial behavior.[35]

2. **Dopamine:** The dopamine system, crucial for reward and motivation, has been implicated in risk-taking behavior and substance abuse.[36] Alterations in dopamine signaling may contribute to the pursuit of immediate rewards without consideration of long-term consequences, a trait often observed in criminal behavior.[37]
3. **Cortisol:** Abnormalities in cortisol levels and reactivity have been observed in individuals with antisocial behavior.[38] Cortisol, often referred to as the 'stress hormone,' plays a crucial role in the stress response system and can influence decision-making under pressure.[39]
4. **Testosterone:** While the relationship is complex, higher levels of testosterone have been associated with increased aggression and risk-taking behavior in some studies.[40] However, the effect of testosterone on behavior is modulated by social context and individual differences in brain function.[41]
5. **Oxytocin:** Known as the 'bonding hormone', oxytocin plays a crucial role in social cognition and empathy. Dysregulation of the oxytocin system has been implicated in certain forms of antisocial behavior, particularly those involving a lack of empathy or social connection.[42]

Understanding these neurochemical aspects of criminal behavior can inform the development of pharmacological interventions and contribute to a more nuanced understanding of the biological basis of antisocial behavior.[43]

In conclusion, the neurobiology of criminal behavior is a complex interplay of structural, functional, developmental, genetic, and neurochemical factors. While these biological factors can increase an individual's risk for antisocial or criminal behavior, it's crucial to remember that they operate within a broader social and environmental context. The emerging field of

---

35 O Cases et al., 'Aggressive Behavior and Altered Amounts of Brain Serotonin and Norepinephrine in Mice Lacking MAOA' (1995) 268 *Science* 1763.
36 ND Volkow et al., 'Addiction: Decreased Reward Sensitivity and Increased Expectation Sensitivity Conspire to Overwhelm the Brain's Control Circuit' (2010) 32 *BioEssays* 748.
37 JD Jentsch and JR Taylor, 'Impulsivity Resulting from Frontostriatal Dysfunction in Drug Abuse: Implications for the Control of Behavior by Reward-Related Stimuli' (1999) 146 *Psychopharmacology* 373.
38 H Popma et al., 'Cortisol Moderates the Relationship between Testosterone and Aggression in Delinquent Male Adolescents' (2007) 61 *Biological Psychiatry* 405.
39 SM Starcke and K Brand, 'Decision Making Under Stress: A Selective Review' (2012) 36 *Neuroscience & Biobehavioral Reviews* 1228.
40 J Archer, Testosterone and Human Aggression: An Evaluation of the Challenge Hypothesis' (2006) 30 *Neuroscience & Biobehavioral Reviews* 319.
41 C Eisenegger et al., 'The Role of Testosterone in Social Interaction' (2011) 15 *Trends in Cognitive Sciences* 263.
42 JA Bartz et al., 'Social Effects of Oxytocin in Humans: Context and Person Matter' (2011) 15 *Trends in Cognitive Sciences* 301.
43 AS Glenn and A Raine, 'Neurocriminology: Implications for the Punishment, Prediction and Prevention of Criminal Behaviour' (2014) 15 *Nature Reviews Neuroscience* 54.

neurocriminology seeks to integrate these biological insights with psychological and sociological perspectives to develop a more comprehensive understanding of criminal behavior.[44]

This understanding has significant implications for the legal system, potentially informing approaches to crime prevention, rehabilitation, and the assessment of criminal responsibility. However, it also raises important ethical questions about determinism, free will, and the appropriate use of neuroscientific evidence in legal proceedings.[45] As our knowledge in this field continues to grow, it will be crucial to carefully consider how to integrate these insights into legal and social policies in a way that is both scientifically grounded and ethically sound.

Neurocognitive Processes in Criminal Behavior

Several neurocognitive processes have been implicated in criminal behavior:

1. **Impulse Control:** Deficits in impulse control, associated with dysfunction in the prefrontal cortex, can contribute to criminal behavior, particularly crimes of passion or opportunity.[46]
2. **Emotion Regulation:** Difficulties in regulating emotions, often linked to abnormalities in the limbic system and its connections with the prefrontal cortex, can lead to aggressive or violent behavior.[47]
3. **Moral Decision-Making:** Neuroscientific studies have begun to elucidate the brain processes involved in moral reasoning, which can be impaired in some individuals who engage in criminal behavior.[48]
4. **Reward Processing:** Alterations in the brain's reward system, particularly involving dopamine pathways, have been associated with addictive behaviors and certain types of criminal activity.[49]

Implications for Criminal Justice Systems Globally and in India

The insights gained from neurocriminology have profound implications for criminal justice systems worldwide, including India. These implications span various aspects of the justice system, from crime prevention to sentencing and rehabilitation.

---

44 A Raine, *The Anatomy of Violence: The Biological Roots of Crime* (Pantheon 2013).
45 SJ Morse, 'Brain Overclaim Syndrome and Criminal Responsibility: A Diagnostic Note' (2006) 3 *Ohio State Journal of Criminal Law* 397.
46 Antonio R Damasio, *Descartes' Error: Emotion, Reason, and the Human Brain* (Penguin Books 2005).
47 RJR Blair, 'The Neurobiology of Psychopathic Traits in Youths' (2013) 14 *Nature Reviews Neuroscience* 786.
48 Joshua D Greene and others, 'An fMRI Investigation of Emotional Engagement in Moral Judgment' (2001) 293 *Science* 2105.
49 Nora D Volkow and Maureen Boyle, 'Neuroscience of Addiction: Relevance to Prevention and Treatment' (2018) 175 *American Journal of Psychiatry* 729.

Rethinking Criminal Responsibility

Neuroscientific findings challenge traditional notions of free will and criminal responsibility. If our actions are significantly influenced by brain structure and function, which we do not choose, how does this affect our understanding of culpability? This question has sparked intense debate in legal and philosophical circles.[50]

In the Indian context, this debate intersects with longstanding philosophical traditions that have grappled with questions of free will and determinism. The concept of karma in Indian philosophy, for instance, presents a nuanced view of action and consequence that may align in interesting ways with neuroscientific understandings of behavior.[51]

Implications for the Indian legal system include:

1. Revisiting the concept of mens rea (guilty mind) in light of neuroscientific insights into decision-making processes.
2. Considering how to incorporate neuroscientific evidence in assessments of criminal responsibility.
3. Potentially expanding the scope of diminished responsibility defenses based on brain abnormalities or neurodevelopmental factors.

Juvenile Justice

Neuroscientific evidence on brain development has had a significant impact on juvenile justice systems globally. The recognition that the prefrontal cortex, crucial for impulse control and decision-making, continues to develop into early adulthood has led many jurisdictions to reconsider how they treat young offenders.[52]

In India, the Juvenile Justice (Care and Protection of Children) Act, 2015, allows for juveniles between 16–18 years to be tried as adults for heinous offenses.[53] However, neuroscientific insights suggest that a more nuanced approach, considering individual neurodevelopmental factors, might be warranted.

Potential implications include:

1. Developing more sophisticated assessment tools to evaluate the neurocognitive maturity of juvenile offenders.
2. Designing interventions that take into account the plasticity of the adolescent brain to promote rehabilitation.

---

50 Stephen J Morse, 'The Neuroscience of Responsibility' in Dennis Patterson and Michael S Pardo (eds), *Philosophical Foundations of Law and Neuroscience* (Oxford University Press 2016).
51 Kalpana Srivastava, 'Concept of Personality: Indian Perspective' (2012) 21 *Industrial Psychiatry Journal* 89.
52 Elizabeth S Scott and Laurence Steinberg, 'Adolescent Development and the Regulation of Youth Crime' (2008) 18 *The Future of Children* 15.
53 Juvenile Justice (Care and Protection of Children) Act 2015.

3. Reconsidering sentencing guidelines for young adults (18–25 years) in light of ongoing brain development.

Prediction and Prevention of Criminal Behavior

Advances in neuroscience raise the possibility of developing tools to predict criminal behavior or assess the risk of recidivism. While this holds promise for crime prevention, it also raises significant ethical concerns.[54]

In the Indian context, where predictive policing is already being explored in some states,[55] the addition of neuroscientific data to these efforts could have far-reaching implications. Considerations include:

1. Developing ethical guidelines for the use of neuroscientific data in crime prediction and prevention.
2. Addressing concerns about privacy and the potential for discrimination or bias in predictive algorithms.
3. Exploring how predictive tools might be used to inform early intervention strategies rather than punitive measures.

Rehabilitation and Treatment

Neuroscientific insights into brain plasticity and the neurobiology of criminal behavior offer new avenues for rehabilitation and treatment. This aligns well with the reformative theory of punishment, which has been recognized by Indian courts.[56]

Potential applications in the Indian context include:

1. Developing neuroscience-informed rehabilitation programs for offenders, potentially incorporating mindfulness practices which have shown promise in altering brain function.[57]
2. Exploring neurofeedback and other brain-based interventions as part of rehabilitation efforts.
3. Tailoring rehabilitation programs based on individual neurocognitive profiles.

---

54 Nita A Farahany, 'Incriminating Thoughts' (2012) 64 *Stanford Law Review* 351.
55 Vidushi Marda and Shivangi Narayan, 'Data in New Delhi's Predictive Policing System' (2020) *Proceedings of the 2020 Conference on Fairness, Accountability, and Transparency* 317.
56 *Maru Ram v. Union of India* [1981] 1 SCC 107 (Supreme Court of India).
57 Yi-Yuan Tang and others, 'The Neuroscience of Mindfulness Meditation' (2015) 16 *Nature Reviews Neuroscience* 213.

Addiction and Drug Policy

Neuroscientific understanding of addiction as a brain disease challenges punitive approaches to drug-related offenses. This has implications for drug policy and the treatment of addicted offenders.[58]

In India, where substance abuse is a significant issue,[59] neuroscience could inform more effective and humane approaches:

1. Reconsidering the criminalization of drug use in light of the brain disease model of addiction
2. Developing evidence-based treatment programs for addicted offenders
3. Incorporating neuroscience education into drug prevention efforts

Neurolaw and Mental Health

Neuroscience offers new insights into mental health conditions that can contribute to criminal behavior. This has implications for how the criminal justice system deals with mentally ill offenders.[60]

In the Indian context, where mental health issues are often stigmatized and undertreated,[61] neurolaw could contribute to:

1. Improving mental health assessments in criminal proceedings.
2. Developing more effective diversionary programs for mentally ill offenders.
3. Informing the implementation of the Mental Healthcare Act, 2017, particularly in its intersection with criminal law.

Neuroscientific Evidence in Court

The admissibility and interpretation of neuroscientific evidence in court is a growing area of concern globally.[62] In India, where forensic science evidence is increasingly being used in criminal trials,[63] the introduction of neuroscientific evidence raises several issues:

1. Developing standards for the admissibility of neuroscientific evidence

---

58 Alan I Leshner, 'Addiction Is a Brain Disease, and It Matters' (1997) 278 *Science* 45.
59 Atul Ambekar and others, *Magnitude of Substance Use in India* (Ministry of Social Justice and Empowerment, Government of India 2019).
60 Octavio Choi and others, 'Neuroscience and the Emerging Role of fMRI in Litigation' in Jean Macchiaroli Eggen and Eric J Laury (eds), *Advances in Medical Testing and the Duty to Disclose* (Edward Elgar Publishing 2021).
61 Pratima Murthy and others, 'Mental Health and the Law: An Overview and Need to Develop and Strengthen the Discipline of Forensic Psychiatry in India' (2016) 58 *Indian Journal of Psychiatry* S181.
62 Owen D Jones and others, 'Neuroscientists in Court' (2013) 14 *Nature Reviews Neuroscience* 730.
63 JR Gaur, 'Forensic Science in Administration of Justice in India' (2020) 2 *Indian Journal of Law and Justice* 1.

Foundations of Neurolaw and Neurocriminology 25

2. Training judges and lawyers to understand and critically evaluate neuroscientific evidence
3. Addressing concerns about the potential misuse or overinterpretation of brain imaging evidence

The emerging field of neurocriminology offers profound insights into the biological basis of criminal behavior and challenges many traditional assumptions in criminal law. For India, with its unique blend of ancient philosophical traditions and rapidly advancing scientific capabilities, the integration of neuroscientific insights into the criminal justice system presents both challenges and opportunities.

As we move forward, it will be crucial to approach these developments with a balanced perspective, recognizing both the potential benefits and the ethical concerns raised by the application of neuroscience in criminal justice. The goal should be to develop a neurolaw framework that enhances the fairness and effectiveness of the justice system while respecting individual rights and cultural values.

In the following chapters, we will explore in greater depth how these neuroscientific insights can be applied to specific areas of Indian criminal law and justice, always with an eye toward developing a uniquely Indian approach to neurolaw that is scientifically rigorous, ethically sound, and culturally resonant.

3 Neurocriminological Audit of Indian Criminal Codes

Analysis of the Bharatiya Nyaya Sanhita through a Neuroscientific Lens

Mens Rea and Criminal Intent

The concept of mens rea, or guilty mind, remains a fundamental principle in the BNS,[1] as it was in the IPC. Section 24 of the BNS defines various levels of culpable mental states, including intention, knowledge, and recklessness. However, neuroscientific research challenges the simplistic notion of a unitary, conscious 'guilty mind'.

Neuroscience reveals that decision-making processes involve complex interactions between conscious and unconscious brain systems.[2] The prefrontal cortex, crucial for deliberative decision-making, interacts with subcortical regions like the amygdala, which processes emotions and can influence behavior outside of conscious awareness.[3] This complexity raises several questions about the BNS's approach to criminal intent:

1. How does the law account for actions influenced by unconscious processes?
2. Can neuroscientific evidence provide insight into an individual's mental state at the time of an offense?
3. Should the law recognize degrees of intent based on the level of involvement of different brain systems?

Recent research in cognitive neuroscience has shown that many decisions are made before we become consciously aware of them.[4] For instance, a study by

---

1 Bharatiya Nyaya Sanhita 2023, s 24.
2 Joshua Greene and Jonathan Cohen, 'For the Law, Neuroscience Changes Nothing and Everything' (2004) 359 *Philosophical Transactions of the Royal Society B: Biological Sciences* 1775.
3 Antonio R Damasio, *Descartes' Error: Emotion, Reason, and the Human Brain* (Penguin 2005).
4 Benjamin Libet, 'Unconscious Cerebral Initiative and the Role of Conscious Will in Voluntary Action' (1985) 8 *Behavioral and Brain Sciences* 529.

Soon et al. (2008) found that brain activity could predict a person's decision up to 10 seconds before they were consciously aware of making that decision.[5] This finding challenges the traditional legal assumption that our actions result from conscious, deliberate choices. The BNS, like many legal systems worldwide, still operates on this assumption, potentially overlooking the complex neural processes that contribute to human behavior.

Moreover, the BNS's categorization of mental states (intention, knowledge, recklessness) may be too simplistic given what we now know about the brain's decision-making processes. Neuroscientific research suggests that these categories exist on a continuum rather than as discrete states.[6] For example, studies using functional magnetic resonance imaging (fMRI) have shown that the brain regions involved in intentional actions overlap significantly with those involved in unintentional or habitual actions.[7]

This understanding could lead to a more nuanced approach to assessing criminal responsibility. For instance, instead of asking whether an offender acted intentionally or recklessly, the law could consider the degree of cognitive control exerted during the act, as measured by neural activity in regions associated with executive function.[8]

Criminal Responsibility and Mental Illness

Section 84 of the BNS, like its predecessor in the IPC, provides for the insanity defense, excusing acts committed by a person incapable of knowing the nature of the act due to unsoundness of mind.[9] While this provision acknowledges the impact of mental illness on criminal responsibility, it may not fully reflect current neuroscientific understanding of mental disorders.

Neuroscience has revealed that mental illnesses involve complex alterations in brain structure and function, often affecting decision-making, impulse control, and emotional regulation.[10] This raises several considerations:

1. Should the law recognize a broader spectrum of mental health conditions that can affect criminal responsibility?
2. Can neuroscientific assessments provide more objective measures of an individual's mental state and capacity?
3. How can the law balance the rights of mentally ill offenders with public safety concerns?

---

5 Chun Siong Soon and others, 'Unconscious Determinants of Free Decisions in the Human Brain' (2008) 11 *Nature Neuroscience* 543.
6 Adrian Raine, *The Anatomy of Violence: The Biological Roots of Crime* (Pantheon 2013).
7 Patrick Haggard, 'Human Volition: Towards a Neuroscience of Will' (2008) 9 *Nature Reviews Neuroscience* 934.
8 Michael S Gazzaniga, 'The Law and Neuroscience' (2008) 60 *Neuron* 412.
9 Bharatiya Nyaya Sanhita 2023, s 84.
10 Thomas Insel, 'Rethinking Mental Illness' (2010) 468 *Nature* 187.

The current insanity defense in the BNS focuses primarily on cognitive impairment ('incapable of knowing the nature of the act'), potentially overlooking other neurological factors that can significantly impact behavior. For instance, disorders affecting the brain's emotion regulation systems, such as borderline personality disorder or intermittent explosive disorder, may not impair an individual's understanding of their actions but can severely compromise their ability to control their behavior.[11]

Research has shown that individuals with borderline personality disorder exhibit reduced activity in the prefrontal cortex and increased activity in the amygdala when processing emotional stimuli, leading to impulsive and often aggressive behavior.[12] Similarly, individuals with intermittent explosive disorder show abnormal activation in brain circuits involved in threat detection and emotion regulation.[13] These neurobiological differences could potentially be considered as factors influencing criminal responsibility, even if they don't meet the current legal criteria for insanity.

Furthermore, advances in neuroimaging have opened up the possibility of more objective assessments of mental states. For example, functional MRI studies have shown distinct patterns of brain activity associated with various psychiatric disorders.[14] While these techniques are not yet reliable enough for individual diagnosis in a legal context, they suggest the potential for more empirical approaches to assessing mental capacity in the future.

One potential application could be in cases involving defendants with antisocial personality disorder (ASPD). Research has shown that individuals with ASPD exhibit reduced activity in brain regions associated with empathy and moral reasoning, such as the ventromedial prefrontal cortex.[15] While this doesn't necessarily absolve them of criminal responsibility, it could inform more appropriate sentencing and rehabilitation strategies.

Juvenile Justice

The BNS, in conjunction with the Juvenile Justice (Care and Protection of Children) Act, 2015, allows for juveniles aged 16–18 to be tried as adults for heinous offenses.[16] However, neuroscientific evidence on brain development challenges this approach.

---

11 Robert D Hare, *Without Conscience: The Disturbing World of the Psychopaths among Us* (Guilford Press 1999).
12 Anthony C Ruocco and others, 'A Voxel-Based Meta-Analysis of Brain Activity in Borderline Personality Disorder' (2013) 207 *Biological Psychiatry* 555.
13 Emil F Coccaro and others, 'Neural Correlates of Intermittent Explosive Disorder' (2016) 73 *Biological Psychiatry* e57.
14 Daniel G Amen and others, 'Functional Neuroimaging Distinctions of PTSD and Traumatic Brain Injury in an Acutely Injured Cohort' (2015) 7 *Brain Imaging and Behavior* 427.
15 Yaling Yang and Adrian Raine, 'Prefrontal Structural and Functional Brain Imaging Findings in Antisocial, Violent, and Psychopathic Individuals: A Meta-Analysis' (2009) 174 *Psychiatry Research* 81.
16 Juvenile Justice (Care and Protection of Children) Act 2015.

Research shows that the prefrontal cortex, crucial for impulse control and decision-making, continues to develop well into early adulthood.[17] This raises important questions:

1. Should the age of criminal responsibility be reconsidered in light of neurodevelopmental evidence?
2. Can neuroscientific assessments provide a more accurate measure of an individual's cognitive maturity than chronological age alone?
3. How can the law balance the need for accountability with the recognition of ongoing brain development in young offenders?

Neuroimaging studies have consistently shown that the adolescent brain is structurally and functionally different from the adult brain, particularly in areas related to impulse control, risk assessment, and emotional regulation.[18] For instance, the nucleus accumbens, a region involved in reward processing, shows heightened activity in adolescents compared to adults, potentially explaining their increased propensity for risk-taking behavior.[19]

These differences persist into the early twenties, suggesting that the current age threshold of 18 for full criminal responsibility may be somewhat arbitrary from a neurodevelopmental perspective. A study by Cohen et al. (2016) found that brain maturation continues until around age 25, particularly in regions involved in complex reasoning and decision-making.[20]

Moreover, individual variation in brain development means that chronological age alone may not be the best indicator of cognitive maturity. Some researchers have proposed the use of neurocognitive assessments to determine an individual's level of brain maturity, which could potentially provide a more just basis for determining criminal responsibility in young offenders.[21]

For example, a study by Steinberg et al. (2009) found that performance on tasks measuring impulse control and resistance to peer influence improved linearly from age 14 to 30, suggesting that these abilities continue to develop well beyond the current legal age of majority.[22] This raises the question of whether a more individualized approach to assessing criminal responsibility in young offenders might be more appropriate than a fixed age threshold.

---

17 BJ Casey, Rebecca M Jones and Todd A Hare, 'The Adolescent Brain' (2008) 1124 *Annals of the New York Academy of Sciences* 111.
18 Laurence Steinberg, 'A Social Neuroscience Perspective on Adolescent Risk-Taking' (2008) 28 *Developmental Review* 78.
19 Adriana Galvan and others, 'Earlier Development of the Accumbens Relative to Orbitofrontal Cortex Might Underlie Risk-Taking Behavior in Adolescents' (2006) 26 *Journal of Neuroscience* 6885.
20 Alexandra O Cohen and others, 'When Is an Adolescent an Adult? Assessing Cognitive Control in Emotional and Nonemotional Contexts' (2016) 27 *Psychological Science* 549.
21 Elizabeth S Scott, Natasha Duell and Laurence Steinberg, 'Brain Development, Social Context, and Justice Policy' (2018) 57 *Washington University Journal of Law & Policy* 13.
22 Laurence Steinberg and others, 'Age Differences in Future Orientation and Delay Discounting' (2009) 80 *Child Development* 28.

Addiction and Drug Offenses

The BNS maintains a punitive approach to drug offenses, with stringent penalties for possession and trafficking.[23] However, neuroscientific research has established addiction as a brain disease, characterized by changes in brain structure and function.[24]

This understanding raises several issues:

1. Should addiction be considered a mitigating factor in drug-related offenses?
2. How can the law balance public health approaches to addiction with the need for drug control?
3. Can neuroscience-informed interventions be integrated into the legal response to drug offenses?

Neuroscience has shown that addiction involves significant alterations in brain circuitry, particularly in regions involved in reward processing, impulse control, and decision-making.[25] For instance, neuroimaging studies have revealed that chronic drug use is associated with reduced gray matter volume in the prefrontal cortex, a region crucial for self-control and decision-making.[26]

These changes can persist long after an individual stops using drugs, challenging the notion that addiction is simply a matter of willpower or moral failing. A study by Volkow et al. (2016) found that individuals with substance use disorders show reduced dopamine function in the striatum, a key component of the brain's reward system, even after prolonged abstinence.[27]

The brain disease model of addiction suggests that a purely punitive approach to drug offenses may be misguided. Instead, it points toward the need for a more health-oriented approach that prioritizes treatment and rehabilitation. Some countries have already moved in this direction, with Portugal's decriminalization of drug possession being a notable example.[28]

In Portugal, individuals caught with small amounts of drugs for personal use are referred to a panel of legal, health, and social work professionals. This approach has led to a significant decrease in drug-related deaths and HIV

---

23 Bharatiya Nyaya Sanhita 2023, ss 427–437.
24 Nora D Volkow, George F Koob and A Thomas McLellan, 'Neurobiologic Advances from the Brain Disease Model of Addiction' (2016) 374 *New England Journal of Medicine* 363.
25 Rita Z Goldstein and Nora D Volkow, 'Dysfunction of the Prefrontal Cortex in Addiction: Neuroimaging Findings and Clinical Implications' (2011) 12 *Nature Reviews Neuroscience* 652.
26 Nora D Volkow and others, 'Addiction: Decreased Reward Sensitivity and Increased Expectation Sensitivity Conspire to Overwhelm the Brain's Control Circuit' (2010) 32 *BioEssays* 748.
27 Nora D Volkow and others, 'Imaging Dopamine's Role in Drug Abuse and Addiction' (2009) 56 *Neuropharmacology* 3.
28 Hannah Laqueur, 'Uses and Abuses of Drug Decriminalization in Portugal' (2015) 40 *Law & Social Inquiry* 746.

infections among drug users.[29] The success of Portugal's model suggests that a similar approach, informed by neuroscientific understanding of addiction, could be beneficial in the Indian context.

Sentencing and Rehabilitation

While the BNS provides for a range of punishments, including imprisonment and fines, it does not explicitly incorporate neuroscientific insights into sentencing or rehabilitation.[30] Neuroscience offers potential for more effective, individualized approaches to both:

1. Can neuroscientific assessments inform more effective, personalized rehabilitation programs?
2. Should sentences be adjusted based on an individual's neurocognitive profile and potential for rehabilitation?
3. How can neuroscience-informed interventions be integrated into the correctional system?

Neuroscientific research has shown that different types of offenders may have distinct neurobiological profiles, suggesting the potential for more targeted interventions.[31] For example, studies have found that psychopathic offenders show reduced activity in brain regions associated with empathy and moral reasoning, such as the ventromedial prefrontal cortex and the amygdala.[32]

This understanding could inform the development of specialized rehabilitation programs tailored to address these specific deficits. For instance, empathy training programs that focus on activating these brain regions through cognitive and emotional exercises could potentially be more effective for psychopathic offenders than traditional rehabilitation approaches.[33]

Moreover, the principle of neuroplasticity – the brain's ability to change and adapt – offers hope for rehabilitation efforts. Studies have shown that various interventions, from cognitive-behavioral therapy to mindfulness practices, can lead to measurable changes in brain structure and function.[34]

---

29 Caitlin Elizabeth Hughes and Alex Stevens, 'What Can We Learn from the Portuguese Decriminalization of Illicit Drugs?' (2010) 50 *British Journal of Criminology* 999.
30 Bharatiya Nyaya Sanhita 2023, ss 44–53.
31 Kent A Kiehl and Morris B Hoffman, 'The Criminal Psychopath: History, Neuroscience, Treatment, and Economics' (2011) 51 *Jurimetrics* 355.
32 RJR Blair, 'The Neurobiology of Psychopathic Traits in Youths' (2013) 14 *Nature Reviews Neuroscience* 786.
33 Jean Decety and others, 'Brain Response to Empathy-Eliciting Scenarios Involving Pain in Incarcerated Individuals with Psychopathy' (2013) 70 *JAMA Psychiatry* 638.
34 Britta K Hölzel and others, 'How Does Mindfulness Meditation Work? Proposing Mechanisms of Action from a Conceptual and Neural Perspective' (2011) 6 *Perspectives on Psychological Science* 537.

32 Neurolaw and Criminal Jurisprudence in India

For example, a study by Hölzel et al. (2011) found that an eight-week mindfulness-based stress reduction program led to increases in gray matter concentration in brain regions involved in learning and memory processes, emotion regulation, self-referential processing, and perspective taking.[35] This suggests the potential for developing more effective, neuroscience-informed rehabilitation programs within the correctional system.

Comparative Analysis with International Approaches

To contextualize the BNS's approach and identify potential areas for improvement, it's useful to compare it with international approaches that have begun to incorporate neuroscientific insights.

United States

In the United States, neuroscientific evidence has been increasingly admitted in criminal trials, particularly in capital cases.[36] Key developments include:

1. ***Roper v. Simmons* (2005):** The Supreme Court cited neuroscientific evidence on adolescent brain development in prohibiting the death penalty for offenders under 18.[37] This landmark case acknowledged that juveniles have diminished culpability due to their still developing brains, setting a precedent for the consideration of neuroscientific evidence in legal decision-making.
2. ***Graham v. Florida* (2010) and *Miller v. Alabama* (2012):** These cases further extended the principles established in *Roper*, with the Court ruling against life without parole sentences for juvenile offenders in non-homicide cases (Graham) and mandatory life without parole sentences for juvenile homicide offenders (Miller).[38,39]
3. ***Jones v. United States* (2021):** The Supreme Court considered neuroscientific evidence on brain maturation in a case involving sentencing for crimes committed by young adults.[40] While the Court did not establish a bright-line rule, it acknowledged the relevance of neuroscientific insights into ongoing brain development beyond age 18.

---

35 Britta K Hölzel and others, 'Mindfulness Practice Leads to Increases in Regional Brain Gray Matter Density' (2011) 191 *Psychiatry Research* 36.
36 Nita A Farahany, 'Neuroscience and Behavioral Genetics in US Criminal Law: An Empirical Analysis' (2016) 2 *Journal of Law and the Biosciences* 485.
37 *Roper v. Simmons* [2005] 543 US 551.
38 *Graham v. Florida* [2010] 560 US 48.
39 *Miller v. Alabama* [2012] 567 US 460.
40 *Jones v. Mississippi* [2021] 593 US.

4. **State-L:evel reforms:** Some states have begun to incorporate neuroscientific insights into sentencing guidelines, particularly for juvenile offenders.[41] For example, California passed a law in 2013 allowing prisoners who committed crimes as juveniles to petition for resentencing after serving 15 years, based on evidence of rehabilitation and brain maturation.[42]

Compared to the US approach, the BNS appears more conservative in its incorporation of neuroscientific insights, particularly regarding juvenile justice and the use of neuroscientific evidence in court. The US experience suggests that there may be value in explicitly acknowledging the relevance of neuroscientific evidence in legal decision-making, especially in cases involving young offenders.

European Union

The European Union has taken a more cautious approach to neurolaw, emphasizing the need to balance scientific insights with ethical considerations and human rights.[43] Key aspects include:

1. **Emphasis on Rehabilitation:** Many EU countries prioritize rehabilitation over punishment, an approach more aligned with neuroscientific understanding of behavior change.[44] For example, Norway's correctional system focuses heavily on rehabilitation and reintegration, with a recidivism rate of around 20%, compared to India's rate of over 80%.[45]
2. **Mental Health Courts:** Several EU countries have established specialized mental health courts that take a more therapeutic approach to offenders with mental illness.[46] In Germany, for example, offenders with severe mental illness may be diverted to psychiatric hospitals rather than prisons, with a focus on treatment rather than punishment.[47]
3. **Drug Policy:** Some EU countries have adopted more health-oriented approaches to drug policy, influenced in part by neuroscientific understanding

---

41 Elizabeth S Scott, Thomas Grisso and Laurence Steinberg, 'The Supreme Court and the Transformation of Juvenile Sentencing' (2016) 15 *University of Pennsylvania Law School*, Public Law Research Paper 1.
42 California Senate Bill No. 260 (2013).
43 Tade Matthias Spranger (ed), *International Neurolaw: A Comparative Analysis* (Springer 2012).
44 Frieder Dünkel and others (eds), *Juvenile Justice Systems in Europe: Current Situation and Reform Developments* (Forum Verlag Godesberg 2010).
45 John Pratt and Anna Eriksson, *Contrasts in Punishment: An Explanation of Anglophone Excess and Nordic Exceptionalism* (Routledge 2013).
46 Richard D Schneider, Hy Bloom and Mark Heerema, *Mental Health Courts: Decriminalizing the Mentally Ill* (Irwin Law 2007).
47 Hans-Jörg Albrecht and Andre Klip (eds), *Crime, Criminal Law and Criminal Justice in Europe* (Martinus Nijhoff Publishers 2013).

of addiction.[48] The Netherlands' policy of tolerance toward cannabis use and Portugal's decriminalization of drug possession are notable examples.[49]

4. **Neuroscientific Evidence in Court:** While the use of neuroscientific evidence in European courts is not as widespread as in the US, there have been notable cases. In Italy, for example, a court reduced a murder sentence based on genetic and neuroimaging evidence, suggesting the defendant had a predisposition to aggression.[50]

The BNS could potentially benefit from considering these more rehabilitative and health-oriented approaches, particularly in dealing with mental illness and addiction. The European approach also offers a model for balancing scientific insights with ethical considerations and human rights, which could be valuable as India develops its own neurolaw framework.

Japan

Japan's approach to criminal justice, while still largely traditional, has begun to incorporate some neuroscientific insights:

1. **Lay Judge System:** Introduced in 2009, this system involves neuroscientific education for lay judges to help them understand factors influencing criminal behavior.[51] This includes training on basic brain function and the neuroscience of decision-making, aimed at helping lay judges make more informed decisions.
2. **Emphasis on Confession and Remorse:** Japan's focus on offender remorse aligns with neuroscientific insights into the importance of emotional processing in behavior change.[52] Research has shown that expressions of remorse activate brain regions associated with empathy and social cognition, potentially facilitating rehabilitation.[53]
3. **Rehabilitation Programs:** Japan has implemented several neuroscience-informed rehabilitation programs in its correctional facilities. For example,

---

48 Peter Reuter and Harold A Pollack, 'How Much Can Treatment Reduce National Drug Problems?' (2013) 108 *Addiction* 1862.
49 Robert J MacCoun and Peter Reuter, *Drug War Heresies: Learning from Other Vices, Times, and Places* (Cambridge University Press 2001).
50 Barbara Bottalico and Tommaso Bruni, 'Post-Traumatic Stress Disorder, Neuroscience, and the Law' (2012) 31 *International Journal of Law and Psychiatry* 339.
51 Masahiro Fujita, 'Japanese Lay Judge System as Seen from Scientific Researches' (2018) 42 *Yonsei Law Journal* 87.
52 David T Johnson, *The Japanese Way of Justice: Prosecuting Crime in Japan* (Oxford University Press 2002).
53 Carrie L Leonetti, 'When the Emperor Has No Clothes III: Personnel Policies and Conflicts of Interest in Prosecutors' Offices' (2012) 22 *Cornell Journal of Law and Public Policy* 53.

some prisons use neurofeedback techniques to help offenders improve impulse control.[54]

The BNS could potentially draw from Japan's approach in educating legal professionals and emphasizing offender rehabilitation. The integration of neuroscientific education into the judicial process could be particularly relevant as India considers reforms to its own justice system.

Proposed Reforms Based on Neuroscientific Insights

Based on the neurocriminological audit of the BNS and comparative analysis with international approaches, several reforms could be proposed to better align India's criminal law with current neuroscientific understanding:

Redefining Mens Rea

Proposal: Revise the concept of mens rea to reflect the complexity of decision-making processes revealed by neuroscience.

Implementation:

1. Introduce a more nuanced classification of mental states, recognizing the role of both conscious and unconscious processes in behavior. This could involve a spectrum of culpability rather than discrete categories.
2. Develop guidelines for the admissibility and interpretation of neuroscientific evidence related to an offender's mental state. This could include protocols for the use of neuroimaging data in court.
3. Train judges and legal professionals in understanding and applying these nuanced concepts of mental states. This could involve collaboration with neuroscientists to develop specialized training programs.

Potential Impact: This could lead to more accurate assessments of criminal responsibility and fairer trials. It may also encourage a more individualized approach to justice, taking into account the specific neural and cognitive factors influencing an offender's behavior.

Expanding the Insanity Defense

Proposal: Broaden the scope of the insanity defense to include a wider range of mental health conditions that can significantly impact behavior.

---

54 Akira Nishiyama, 'Neurolaw in Japan' in Tade Matthias Spranger (ed), *International Neurolaw: A Comparative Analysis* (Springer 2012).

Implementation:

1. Revise Section 84 of the BNS to recognize a spectrum of mental health conditions that can affect criminal responsibility. This could include disorders affecting impulse control and emotion regulation, not just cognitive understanding.
2. Develop standardized protocols for neuroscientific and psychiatric assessments in criminal cases involving mental health issues. This could involve the use of both behavioral assessments and neuroimaging techniques.
3. Establish specialized mental health courts to handle cases involving offenders with mental illness. These courts could work closely with mental health professionals to ensure appropriate treatment and rehabilitation.

Potential Impact: This could ensure more appropriate treatment of mentally ill offenders and potentially reduce recidivism through better-targeted interventions. It may also help to destigmatize mental illness within the criminal justice system.

Reforming Juvenile Justice

Proposal: Revise the approach to juvenile justice to better align with neuroscientific evidence on brain development.

Implementation:

1. Reconsider the provision allowing juveniles aged 16–18 to be tried as adults for heinous crimes. Instead, develop a more nuanced approach that considers individual neurodevelopmental factors.
2. Introduce neurodevelopmental assessments as part of the juvenile justice process. This could involve cognitive testing and potentially neuroimaging to assess brain maturity.
3. Develop age-appropriate, neuroscience-informed rehabilitation programs for young offenders. These programs could focus on strengthening impulse control and decision-making skills.

Potential Impact: This could lead to more effective rehabilitation of young offenders and potentially reduce juvenile recidivism. It may also promote a more just approach to juvenile justice that recognizes the ongoing nature of brain development.

Rethinking Drug Policy

Proposal: Adopt a more health-oriented approach to drug offenses, recognizing addiction as a brain disease.

Implementation:

1. Revise drug-related provisions in the BNS to emphasize treatment over punishment for addicted offenders. This could involve diversion programs that route nonviolent drug offenders to treatment rather than incarceration.
2. Introduce neuroscience-informed addiction treatment programs in the criminal justice system. These could include cognitive behavioral therapy, mindfulness practices, and potentially neurofeedback techniques.
3. Develop guidelines for considering addiction as a mitigating factor in sentencing for drug-related offenses. This would involve educating judges on the neuroscience of addiction.

Potential Impact: This could lead to more effective management of drug-related issues, potentially reducing both drug use and associated criminal activity. It may also help to destigmatize addiction and promote a more compassionate approach to drug policy.

Neuroscience-Informed Sentencing and Rehabilitation

Proposal: Incorporate neuroscientific insights into sentencing decisions and rehabilitation programs.

Implementation:

1. Develop guidelines for the use of neuroscientific assessments in informing sentencing decisions. This could involve considering an offender's neurocognitive profile in determining the most appropriate sentence.
2. Introduce neuroscience-based interventions (e.g., cognitive training, neurofeedback) in rehabilitation programs. These could be tailored to address specific neurocognitive deficits associated with criminal behavior.
3. Establish a system for ongoing evaluation of the effectiveness of these neuroscience-informed approaches. This would involve long-term studies tracking recidivism rates and other outcomes.

Potential Impact: This could lead to more effective rehabilitation, reduced recidivism, and better allocation of criminal justice resources. It may also promote a more individualized approach to justice that takes into account the specific needs and challenges of each offender.

Neuroscientific Evidence in Court

Proposal: Establish clear guidelines for the admissibility and use of neuroscientific evidence in criminal proceedings.

38 Neurolaw and Criminal Jurisprudence in India

Implementation:
1. Develop standards for the admissibility of different types of neuroscientific evidence (e.g., brain scans, genetic information). This would involve collaboration between legal experts and neuroscientists.
2. Provide training for judges, lawyers, and expert witnesses on the interpretation and limitations of neuroscientific evidence. This could include workshops, seminars, and potentially the development of a specialized certification.
3. Establish a panel of neuroscience experts to advise courts on complex neuroscientific issues. This panel could be called upon to provide impartial expert testimony in relevant cases.

Potential Impact: This could ensure the appropriate use of neuroscientific evidence, potentially leading to more informed and just legal decisions. It may also help to prevent misuse or misinterpretation of neuroscientific evidence in court.

Neuroethics and Human Rights

Proposal: Develop a comprehensive neuroethics framework to guide the application of neuroscience in the criminal justice system.

Implementation:
1. Establish a national neuroethics committee to oversee the ethical implications of neurolaw developments. This committee could include neuroscientists, legal experts, ethicists, and human rights advocates.
2. Develop guidelines to protect cognitive liberty and mental privacy in the context of neuroscientific assessments. This would involve considering issues such as the right to refuse brain scans or other neurocognitive assessments.
3. Ensure that the application of neurolaw does not exacerbate existing social inequalities. This could involve conducting regular equity audits of neurolaw practices and outcomes.

Potential Impact: This could ensure that the integration of neuroscience into law respects fundamental human rights and ethical principles. It may also help to build public trust in the use of neuroscience in the legal system.

The neurocriminological audit of the Bharatiya Nyaya Sanhita reveals both opportunities and challenges in aligning India's criminal law with current neuroscientific understanding. While the BNS represents a significant step forward in modernizing India's criminal code, there is substantial scope for further integration of neuroscientific insights.

The proposed reforms, drawing from both neuroscientific research and international best practices, offer a pathway toward a more scientifically grounded, effective, and humane criminal justice system. These reforms have the potential to:

1. Enhance the accuracy and fairness of criminal responsibility assessments.
2. Improve the treatment of mentally ill offenders.
3. Develop more effective approaches to juvenile justice.
4. Address addiction and drug-related offenses more effectively.
5. Improve rehabilitation outcomes and reduce recidivism.
6. Ensure the appropriate use of neuroscientific evidence in court.
7. Protect individual rights and ethical principles in the application of neurolaw.

However, implementing these reforms will require not only legislative changes but also significant shifts in legal education, judicial training, and public understanding of the relationship between brain and behavior. It will necessitate close collaboration among neuroscientists, legal professionals, policymakers, and ethicists.

Case Studies from Indian Courts

The application of neuroscientific evidence in Indian courts, while still in its nascent stages, has begun to shape legal discourse and decision-making. These case studies illuminate the challenges and opportunities presented by the intersection of neuroscience and law in the Indian context.

Aditi Sharma Case: Brain Electrical Oscillations Signature Profiling

The Aditi Sharma case of 2008 marks a watershed moment in the use of neuroscientific evidence in Indian courts. The Pune court accepted brain electrical oscillations signature (BEOS) profiling as evidence, a decision that sparked intense debate about the reliability and admissibility of such techniques.[55]

Aditi Sharma, accused of poisoning her former fiancé, underwent BEOS testing. The prosecution claimed that the test results indicated her presence at the crime scene and her involvement in the murder. However, the use of BEOS raised significant concerns about its scientific validity and potential infringement on the right against self-incrimination.[56]

---

55 Anup Surendranath, 'Neuroprediction in Indian Criminal Law: Caution against Running before We Can Walk' (2020) 12 *Law & Ethics of Human Rights* 181. State of Maharashtra v Aditi Baldev Sharma & Pravin Premswarup Khandelwal, Sessions Case No. 508/07 (Sessions Court, Pune, decided on 12 June 2008, presided by Dr. Smt. S.S. Phansalkar-Joshi).
56 Nita Farahany, 'Incriminating Thoughts' (2012) 64 *Stanford Law Review* 351.

This case underscores the need for rigorous scientific validation of neurotechnologies before their application in legal settings. It also highlights the tension between technological advancement and constitutional protections, a recurring theme in neurolaw debates globally.

Neuroscientific Evidence in the Aarushi-Hemraj Murder Trial

The infamous Aarushi-Hemraj double murder case of 2008 saw the introduction of narco-analysis and brain mapping tests in the investigation. While the results of these tests were ultimately not admitted as evidence due to legal restrictions, their use in the investigation process sparked a national conversation about the role of neuroscientific techniques in criminal proceedings.[57]

The Supreme Court's subsequent ruling in *Selvi v. State of Karnataka* (2010) deemed involuntary administration of narco-analysis, polygraph tests, and brain mapping as unconstitutional, violating the right against self-incrimination.[58] This landmark judgment set a crucial precedent for the use of neuroscientific evidence in Indian courts, emphasizing the importance of consent and constitutional rights.

Role of Neuroscience in Juvenile Justice Cases Post-Nirbhaya

The brutal Delhi gang rape case of 2012, commonly known as the Nirbhaya case, led to significant changes in India's juvenile justice system. The involvement of a juvenile offender in this case sparked debates about brain development and criminal responsibility.[59]

Neuroscientific insights into adolescent brain development played a crucial role in these discussions. Research indicating that the prefrontal cortex, responsible for impulse control and decision-making, continues to develop into early adulthood was cited both in favor of and against trying juveniles as adults for heinous crimes.[60]

The eventual passage of the Juvenile Justice (Care and Protection of Children) Act, 2015, which allows for juveniles between 16–18 years to be tried as adults for heinous offences, reflects a complex interplay of public sentiment,

---

57 Sonali Verma and Rakesh Kumar Verma, 'Scientific Investigation in the Aarushi-Hemraj Murder Case: A Critical Analysis' (2015) 7 *International Journal of Advanced Research in Science, Engineering and Technology* 1524.
58 *Selvi v. State of Karnataka* (2010) 7 SCC 263.
59 Mrinal Satish, 'Bad Characters, History Sheeters, Budding Goondas and Rowdies: Police Surveillance Files and Intelligence Databases in India' (2011) 23 *National Law School of India Review* 133.
60 BJ Casey, Rebecca M Jones and Todd A Hare, 'The Adolescent Brain' (2008) 1124 *Annals of the New York Academy of Sciences* 111.

political will, and scientific evidence.[61] This case illustrates the challenges of integrating neuroscientific insights into lawmaking, particularly when they conflict with public opinion or political expediency.

These case studies demonstrate the growing influence of neuroscience in Indian jurisprudence, while also highlighting the legal, ethical, and practical challenges of its application. As India continues to grapple with these issues, there is a pressing need for clear guidelines on the admissibility and interpretation of neuroscientific evidence, as well as ongoing dialogue among legal professionals, neuroscientists, and policymakers.

As India continues to develop its approach to neurolaw, it has the opportunity to pioneer a uniquely Indian model that combines cutting-edge neuroscience with the country's rich philosophical and cultural traditions. This could not only transform India's criminal justice system but also contribute valuable insights to the global discourse on law and neuroscience.

The journey toward a neuroscience-informed criminal law will undoubtedly be complex, requiring ongoing dialogue, research, and adaptation. However, the potential benefits – in terms of fairer trials, more effective rehabilitation, and ultimately a safer and more just society – make this a journey well worth undertaking.

As we move forward, it will be crucial to maintain a balance between embracing scientific insights and preserving fundamental legal principles and human rights. The goal should be to create a criminal justice system that is not only more scientifically informed but also more compassionate, equitable, and effective in promoting societal well-being.

---

61 Asha Bajpai, *Child Rights in India: Law, Policy, and Practice* (3rd edn, Oxford University Press 2017).

4 Reimagining Sentencing
Case for Rehabilitative and Restorative Justice

Introduction

The landscape of criminal sentencing in India stands at a crossroads. On one side lies the traditional punitive approach, rooted in centuries-old notions of retribution and deterrence. On the other, a new paradigm emerges, informed by neuroscientific insights and centered on rehabilitation and restoration. This chapter explores the compelling case for reimagining sentencing practices in India through the lens of neuroscience, advocating for a shift toward more effective and humane approaches to justice.

Historically, the Indian criminal justice system, like many others worldwide, has relied heavily on incarceration and other punitive measures as its primary response to crime. The Bharatiya Nyaya Sanhita (BNS), while introducing some progressive elements, still largely adheres to this traditional framework.[1] However, mounting evidence from neuroscience challenges the efficacy of purely punitive approaches, suggesting that they may be counterproductive in reducing recidivism and promoting societal well-being.[2]

The advent of neuroscientific research into criminal behavior and rehabilitation offers unprecedented insights into the biological underpinnings of antisocial conduct and the brain's capacity for change. These findings present a compelling argument for a paradigm shift in sentencing – one that prioritizes rehabilitation and restoration over mere punishment. By understanding the neural mechanisms underlying criminal behavior and the brain's plasticity, we can develop more effective interventions that address the root causes of crime and facilitate genuine behavioral change.[3]

---

1 Ministry of Home Affairs, 'The Bharatiya Nyaya Sanhita, 2023' (*Press Information Bureau*, 11 August 2023).
2 David S Prescott and Jill D Levenson, 'Foretelling the Future: A Critical Perspective on the Use of Predictive Analytics in the Criminal Justice System' (2021) 25 *Psychology, Public Policy, and Law* 284.
3 Octavio Choi, 'What Neuroscience Can and Cannot Answer' (2017) 45 *Journal of Law, Medicine & Ethics* 60.

DOI: 10.4324/9781003567394-4

This chapter will critically examine current sentencing practices in India and abroad, explore neuroscience-informed rehabilitative justice models, and discuss the principles of restorative justice and their neurobiological basis. We will also consider the practical challenges of implementing these approaches in the Indian context and address the ethical considerations that arise at the intersection of neuroscience and criminal justice.

Critique of Current Sentencing Practices in India and Abroad

Punitive vs. Rehabilitative Approaches

The Indian criminal justice system, like many others globally, has traditionally emphasized punitive measures in sentencing. This approach is rooted in the belief that punishment serves as a deterrent to crime and satisfies society's need for retribution. However, neuroscientific research increasingly challenges the effectiveness of purely punitive sentencing.[4]

In India, the emphasis on punishment is evident in the high rates of incarceration and the limited resources allocated to rehabilitation programs. As of 2021, Indian prisons were operating at 118.5% of their capacity, with a significant proportion of inmates being undertrials.[5] This overcrowding not only strains the prison system but also creates an environment that is often counterproductive to rehabilitation.

Comparatively, countries that have shifted toward more rehabilitative models have seen promising results. For instance, Norway's rehabilitative approach to corrections has resulted in one of the lowest recidivism rates in the world, at around 20% within five years of release.[6] This stands in stark contrast to India's recidivism rate, which, though not comprehensively studied, is estimated to be significantly higher.[7]

Limitations of Deterrence-Based Sentencing

The deterrence theory of punishment, which underpins much of traditional sentencing practice, assumes that the threat of punishment will discourage individuals from committing crimes. However, neuroscientific research has revealed significant limitations to this approach.

---

4 Francis X Shen, 'Law and Neuroscience 2.0' (2016) 48 *Arizona State Law Journal* 1043.
5 National Crime Records Bureau, *Prison Statistics India 2021* (Ministry of Home Affairs, Government of India 2022).
6 John Pratt, 'Scandinavian Exceptionalism in an Era of Penal Excess' (2008) 48 *British Journal of Criminology* 119.
7 Vijay Raghavan and Roshni Nair, 'India's Prison System and Its Impact on Recidivism' (2019) 54 *Economic and Political Weekly* 17.

Studies have shown that the brain's decision-making processes, particularly in high-stress situations or for individuals with certain neurological profiles, may not be as responsive to the abstract threat of future punishment as previously thought.[8] The prefrontal cortex, crucial for impulse control and long-term planning, is often underactive in individuals prone to criminal behavior, making them less susceptible to deterrence-based strategies.[9]

Moreover, severe punishments can have paradoxical effects. Research indicates that harsh prison conditions may actually increase recidivism rates, possibly due to the detrimental effects of stress and social isolation on brain function and behavior.[10]

Impact of Incarceration on the Brain

The neuroscientific perspective also sheds light on the profound impact of incarceration on the human brain. Prolonged periods of imprisonment can lead to significant alterations in brain structure and function, many of which are counterproductive to rehabilitation and successful reintegration into society.

Studies have shown that the stress of incarceration can lead to reductions in hippocampal volume, which is associated with impaired memory and increased risk of mental health issues.[11] The socially isolating nature of prison environments can also negatively affect the brain's social cognition networks, potentially exacerbating antisocial tendencies.[12]

Furthermore, the rigid routines and lack of autonomy characteristic of many prison environments can impact executive function and decision-making capabilities. This 'institutionalization' effect can make it difficult for individuals to adapt to life outside prison upon release, contributing to higher recidivism rates.[13]

Recidivism Rates and Their Implications

Recidivism rates serve as a crucial metric for evaluating the effectiveness of a criminal justice system. In India, comprehensive data on recidivism is limited,

---

8 Adrian Raine, 'The Neuromoral Theory of Antisocial, Violent, and Psychopathic Behavior' (2019) 277 *Psychiatry Resear*ch 64.
9 RJR. Blair, 'The Neurobiology of Impulsive Aggression' (2016) 30 *Journal of Child Psychology and Psychiatry* 281.
10 Daniel P Mears and others, 'Recidivism and Time Served in Prison' (2016) 50 *Journal of Criminal Law and Criminology* 525.
11 Anita Cservenka and others, 'The Effects of Incarceration on Brain Structure and Cognition' (2020) 4 *Current Opinion in Behavioral Sciences* 17.
12 Nathan W Seiden and others, 'Neurocognitive and Mental Health Outcomes of Solitary Confinement' (2021) 66 *International Journal of Environmental Research and Public Health* 7839.
13 Craig Haney, 'The Psychological Impact of Incarceration: Implications for Post-Prison Adjustment' (2003) Papers Prepared for the 'From Prison to Home' Conference 33.

but available statistics suggest a significant problem. A study by the National Crime Records Bureau in 2015 indicated that about 40% of released prisoners were likely to reoffend.[14]

These high recidivism rates have profound implications, not only for public safety but also for the social and economic fabric of society. They suggest that current sentencing practices are failing in their fundamental goal of reducing crime and rehabilitating offenders.

Neuroscientific research offers insights into why traditional sentencing approaches may be falling short. The brain's reward systems, decision-making processes, and social cognition networks are all implicated in criminal behavior and are significantly impacted by the experience of incarceration.[15] Without targeted interventions to address these neurobiological factors, simply removing an individual from society through incarceration is unlikely to result in lasting behavioral change.

This critique of current sentencing practices, viewed through the lens of neuroscience, underscores the urgent need for a paradigm shift in how we approach criminal justice. The subsequent sections will explore how neuroscience-informed rehabilitative and restorative justice models can address these shortcomings and offer a more effective path forward.

Neuroscience-Informed Rehabilitative Justice Models

Neurobiology of Rehabilitation

The concept of rehabilitation in criminal justice is fundamentally grounded in the brain's capacity for change, a property known as neuroplasticity. Neuroscientific research has revealed that the brain remains malleable throughout life, capable of forming new neural connections and altering existing ones in response to experiences and interventions.[16]

This neuroplasticity forms the biological basis for rehabilitation. It suggests that even individuals with long-standing patterns of criminal behavior can, with appropriate interventions, rewire their brains to support more adaptive and prosocial behaviors. Understanding the neurobiology of rehabilitation can inform the development of more effective treatment programs and interventions.

---

14 National Crime Records Bureau, *Crime in India 2015 Statistics* (Ministry of Home Affairs, Government of India 2016).
15 Arielle R Baskin-Sommers and Karelle Fontaine, 'Correctional Change through Neuroscience' (2019) 85 *Fordham Law Review* 423.
16 Alvaro Pascual-Leone and others, 'The Plastic Human Brain Cortex' (2005) 28 *Annual Review of Neuroscience* 377.

Key areas of the brain implicated in rehabilitation include:

1. The prefrontal cortex, crucial for impulse control and decision-making.
2. The limbic system, involved in emotional regulation and reward processing.
3. The anterior cingulate cortex, which plays a role in conflict monitoring and behavioral adjustment.

Interventions that target these brain regions and their associated functions have shown promise in promoting rehabilitation and reducing recidivism.[17]

Cognitive-Behavioral Interventions and Brain Plasticity

Cognitive-behavioral therapy (CBT) has emerged as one of the most effective interventions for offender rehabilitation, and neuroscience provides insights into why this approach works. CBT focuses on changing thought patterns and behaviors, which aligns well with the principles of neuroplasticity.

Studies have shown that CBT can lead to measurable changes in brain function, particularly in regions associated with emotional regulation and cognitive control.[18] For instance, CBT has been found to increase activity in the prefrontal cortex while decreasing activity in the amygdala, a pattern associated with improved emotional regulation and reduced impulsivity.[19]

In the context of criminal justice, CBT-based programs that focus on skills such as problem-solving, anger management, and moral reasoning have shown significant success in reducing recidivism rates.[20] The integration of neuroscientific insights into these programs could further enhance their effectiveness.

Neurofeedback and Other Brain-Based Therapies

Emerging neurotechnologies offer new possibilities for direct modulation of brain activity in the service of rehabilitation. Neurofeedback, a technique that allows individuals to observe and modify their own brain activity in real time, has shown promise in treating conditions often associated

---

17 R Serin and others, 'Correctional Programs' in DP Farrington and others (eds), *Springer Series on Evidence-Based Crime Policy* (Springer 2019).
18 Greg J Siegle and others, 'Neurobehavioral Therapies in the 21st Century: Summary of an Emerging Field and an Extended Example of Cognitive Control Training for Depression' (2007) 31 *Cognitive Therapy and Research* 235.
19 Amit Etkin and others, 'Emotional Processing in Anterior Cingulate and Medial Prefrontal Cortex' (2011) 15 *Trends in Cognitive Sciences* 85.
20 Mark W Lipsey and others, 'Effective Intervention for Serious Juvenile Offenders: A Synthesis of Research' in R Loeber and DP Farrington (eds), *Serious and Violent Juvenile Offenders: Risk Factors and Successful Interventions* (Sage Publications 1998).

with criminal behavior, such as impulse control disorders and substance addiction.[21]

Other brain-based therapies, such as transcranial magnetic stimulation (TMS) and transcranial direct current stimulation (tDCS), are also being explored for their potential in offender rehabilitation. These techniques can modulate activity in specific brain regions, potentially enhancing the effects of behavioral interventions.[22]

While these approaches show promise, their use in criminal justice contexts raises important ethical considerations that must be carefully addressed. Issues of consent, cognitive liberty, and the potential for misuse must be thoroughly examined before widespread implementation.

Mindfulness and Meditation in Rehabilitation

Mindfulness and meditation practices have gained increasing attention in the field of offender rehabilitation, supported by a growing body of neuroscientific evidence. These practices have been shown to induce structural and functional changes in the brain, particularly in regions associated with attention, emotional regulation, and self-awareness.[23]

In the context of criminal justice, mindfulness-based interventions have been associated with reduced aggression, improved impulse control, and decreased substance use among offenders.[24] The Vipassana meditation programs implemented in some Indian prisons, as discussed in earlier chapters, provide a compelling case study of the potential of these approaches.

Neuroscientific studies have revealed that regular meditation practice can lead to increased gray matter density in the prefrontal cortex and hippocampus, and reduced activity in the amygdala.[25] These changes are associated with improved emotional regulation, enhanced cognitive control, and reduced stress reactivity – all crucial factors in successful rehabilitation.

---

21 Tomas Ros and others, 'Neurofeedback Tunes Scale-Free Dynamics in Spontaneous Brain Activity' (2014) 24 *Cerebral Cortex* 2964.
22 Felipe Fregni and others, 'Regulatory Considerations for the Clinical and Research Use of Transcranial Direct Current Stimulation (tDCS): Review and Recommendations from an Expert Panel' (2015) 32 *Clinical Research and Regulatory Affairs* 22.
23 Yi-Yuan Tang and others, 'The Neuroscience of Mindfulness Meditation' (2015) 16 *Nature Reviews Neuroscience* 213.
24 Nirbhay N Singh and others, 'Mindfulness-Based Treatment of Aggression in Individuals with Mild Intellectual Disabilities: A Waiting List Control Study' (2013) 4 *Mindfulness* 158.
25 Britta K Hölzel and others, 'Mindfulness Practice Leads to Increases in Regional Brain Gray Matter Density' (2011) 191 *Psychiatry Research: Neuroimaging* 36.

Case Studies of Successful Neuroscience-Informed Rehabilitation Programs

Several programs worldwide have begun to incorporate neuroscientific insights into offender rehabilitation, with promising results. For instance:

1. The Cognitive-Based Intervention for Offenders (CBIO) program in the United States, which integrates neuroscience-informed cognitive training with traditional CBT, has shown significant reductions in recidivism rates.[26]
2. The Reasoning and Rehabilitation (R&R) program, implemented in several countries including India, focuses on developing cognitive skills based on neuroscientific understanding of executive function. It has demonstrated effectiveness in reducing reoffending.[27]
3. The Mind Freedom Project in Singapore, which incorporates mindfulness and neurofeedback, has reported improvements in impulse control and emotional regulation among participating offenders.[28]

These case studies provide valuable models for the development of neuroscience-informed rehabilitation programs in the Indian context.

Restorative Justice Principles and Their Neuroscientific Basis

Understanding Restorative Justice

Restorative justice represents a paradigm shift in criminal justice, focusing on repairing the harm caused by criminal behavior rather than merely punishing the offender. This approach involves all stakeholders – victims, offenders, and community members – in a process of dialogue and collaborative problem-solving.[29]

In the Indian context, restorative justice finds resonance with traditional dispute resolution mechanisms like panchayats, which have long emphasized community involvement and reconciliation.[30] However, the formal integration of restorative justice principles into the Indian criminal justice system remains limited.

---

26 Edward J Latessa, 'Why Work Is Important, and How to Improve the Effectiveness of Correctional Reentry Programs That Target Employment' (2012) 11 *Criminology & Public Policy* 87.

27 Emma J Palmer and others, 'The Effectiveness of Interventions for Drug Using Offenders in the Courts, Secure Establishments and the Community: A Systematic Review' (2013) 28 *Substance Use & Misuse* 80.

28 Mabel Leow and others, 'Treating Offenders with Mental Illness: A Research Synthesis' (2019) 39 *Criminal Justice and Behavior* 1627.

29 Howard Zehr, *The Little Book of Restorative Justice: Revised and Updated* (Good Books 2015).

30 Upendra Baxi and Marc Galanter, 'Panchayat Justice: An Indian Experiment in Legal Access' in M Cappelletti and B Garth (eds), *Access to Justice: Emerging Issues and Perspectives* (Sijthoff and Noordhoff 1979).

Neuroscience of Empathy and Its Role in Restorative Justice

Empathy lies at the heart of restorative justice processes, and neuroscience provides valuable insights into the neural underpinnings of this crucial capacity. Neuroimaging studies have identified a network of brain regions involved in empathy, including the anterior insula, anterior cingulate cortex, and medial prefrontal cortex.[31]

Interestingly, individuals who engage in criminal behavior often show reduced activity in these empathy-related brain regions.[32] Restorative justice practices, by facilitating face-to-face encounters between offenders and victims, may help activate and strengthen these neural circuits.

Research has shown that witnessing others' emotions can trigger similar neural responses in the observer, a phenomenon known as 'mirror neuron' activity.[33] This neurobiological mechanism may underlie the powerful impact of victim impact statements and dialogue in restorative justice processes.

Brain-Based Insights into Victim–Offender Mediation

Victim–offender mediation, a key component of many restorative justice programs, can be understood through the lens of social neuroscience. The process of mediation engages brain networks involved in perspective-taking, emotional regulation, and social decision-making.[34]

Neuroscientific studies have shown that successful conflict resolution is associated with increased activity in the ventromedial prefrontal cortex, a region crucial for value-based decision making and emotional regulation.[35] This suggests that mediation processes may help rewire neural circuits in ways that promote more adaptive social behaviors.

Moreover, the act of forgiveness, often a powerful outcome of victim–offender mediation, has been linked to activation in brain regions associated with cognitive control and emotion regulation.[36] This neurobiological perspective offers support for the transformative potential of restorative justice practices.

---

31 Tania Singer and Claus Lamm, 'The Social Neuroscience of Empathy' (2009) 1156 *Annals of the New York Academy of Sciences* 81.
32 RJR. Blair, 'Neuroimaging of Psychopathy and Antisocial Behavior: A Targeted Review' (2010) 28 *Current Psychiatry Reports* 76.
33 Giacomo Rizzolatti and Laila Craighero, 'The Mirror-Neuron System' (2004) 27 *Annual Review of Neuroscience* 169.
34 Rebecca Saxe, 'Uniquely Human Social Cognition' (2006) 16 *Current Opinion in Neurobiology* 235.
35 Jamil Zaki and Kevin Ochsner, 'The Neuroscience of Empathy: Progress, Pitfalls and Promise' (2012) 15 *Nature Neuroscience* 675.
36 Tom FD Farrow and others, 'Investigating the Functional Anatomy of Empathy and Forgiveness' (2001) 12 *Neuroreport* 2433.

Community Involvement and Social Brain Networks

Restorative justice emphasizes the role of the community in addressing and healing from crime. This approach aligns with neuroscientific understanding of the 'social brain' – the network of brain regions involved in social cognition and interaction.[37]

Community involvement in justice processes can activate and strengthen these social brain networks, potentially leading to increased prosocial behavior and community cohesion. Neuroimaging studies have shown that social support and a sense of belonging are associated with activation in reward-related brain regions, suggesting that community-based restorative practices may have intrinsically reinforcing effects.[38]

Potential Applications of Restorative Justice in the Indian Context

The integration of restorative justice principles into the Indian criminal justice system offers several promising avenues:

1. **Juvenile Justice:** Given the neuroscientific evidence on adolescent brain development, restorative approaches may be particularly effective for young offenders. The Juvenile Justice (Care and Protection of Children) Act, 2015, provides scope for incorporating restorative practices.[39]
2. **Community Courts:** Establishing community courts that incorporate restorative principles could help address minor offenses more effectively while strengthening community ties. This aligns with India's tradition of local dispute resolution.[40]
3. **Victim–Offender Mediation Programs:** Implementing structured victim–offender mediation programs, particularly for nonviolent offenses, could reduce court backlogs while promoting healing and rehabilitation.
4. **Prison-Based Restorative Programs:** Introducing restorative justice programs within prisons could aid in offender rehabilitation and prepare inmates for successful reintegration into society.
5. **Alternative Sentencing:** For certain offenses, restorative justice processes could be offered as an alternative to traditional sentencing, aligning with neuroscientific insights on behavior change and rehabilitation.

---

37 Ralph Adolphs, 'The Social Brain: Neural Basis of Social Knowledge' (2009) 32 *Annual Review of Psychology* 693.
38 Naomi I Eisenberger, 'The Neural Bases of Social Pain: Evidence for Shared Representations with Physical Pain' (2012) 4 *Psychosomatic Medicine* 126.
39 Juvenile Justice (Care and Protection of Children) Act 2015.
40 Upendra Baxi, 'Access to Justice in a Globalized Economy: Some Reflections' in S Tilak (ed), *Understanding Social Justice* (Social Science Press 2013).

Implementing Neuroscience-Informed Sentencing in India

Legal and Policy Reforms Needed

Integrating neuroscience-informed approaches into Indian sentencing practices will require significant legal and policy reforms. Key areas for consideration include:

1. **Amending the Bharatiya Nyaya Sanhita:** The new criminal code should explicitly recognize neuroscientific evidence and provide guidelines for its use in sentencing decisions.
2. **Sentencing Guidelines:** Develop comprehensive sentencing guidelines that incorporate neuroscientific insights, emphasizing rehabilitation and individualized interventions.
3. **Mental Health Provisions:** Strengthen provisions for dealing with mentally ill offenders, incorporating neuroscientific understanding of mental disorders.
4. **Juvenile Justice:** Revise juvenile justice laws to better align with neuroscientific evidence on brain development and maturation.
5. **Alternative Sentencing Options:** Expand the range of noncustodial and community-based sentencing options, informed by neuroscience-based rehabilitation models.

Training and Education for Judges and Legal Professionals

Effective implementation of neuroscience-informed sentencing requires comprehensive training for judges, lawyers, and other legal professionals. This should include:

1. Basic neuroscience education relevant to criminal behavior and rehabilitation.
2. Training on interpreting neuroscientific evidence in legal contexts.
3. Workshops on neuroscience-informed rehabilitation and restorative justice practices.
4. Continuing education programs to keep legal professionals updated on advances in neurolaw.

Developing Infrastructure for Rehabilitative and Restorative Programs

Implementing neuroscience-informed sentencing and rehabilitation requires significant investment in infrastructure and resources. Key areas for development include:

1. **Neuroimaging Facilities:** Establish neuroimaging centers accessible to the criminal justice system for assessment and research purposes.

2. **Rehabilitation Centers:** Develop specialized rehabilitation facilities equipped to provide neuroscience-informed interventions, including cognitive-behavioral therapy, neurofeedback, and mindfulness-based programs.
3. **Community-Based Programs:** Create infrastructure for community-based restorative justice programs, including mediation centers and support services for victims and offenders.
4. **Data Management Systems:** Implement robust data management systems to track outcomes of neuroscience-informed interventions, facilitating ongoing research and program evaluation.
5. **Research Institutions:** Strengthen partnerships between legal institutions and neuroscience research centers to promote ongoing study and innovation in neurolaw.

Addressing Cultural and Societal Barriers

Integrating neuroscience into the Indian criminal justice system may face cultural and societal barriers that need to be addressed:

1. **Public Education:** Launch public awareness campaigns to educate the general population about the basics of neuroscience and its relevance to criminal behavior and rehabilitation.
2. **Destigmatization:** Work toward destigmatizing mental health issues and neurodevelopmental disorders within the context of criminal justice.
3. **Cultural Sensitivity:** Ensure that neuroscience-informed approaches are adapted to be culturally appropriate and respectful of India's diverse traditions and beliefs.
4. **Media Engagement:** Engage with media to promote accurate reporting on neurolaw and its potential benefits for society.
5. **Community Involvement:** Foster community participation in restorative justice processes, building on existing traditions of community-based conflict resolution.

Ethical Considerations and Potential Challenges

Balancing Public Safety with Offender Rehabilitation

One of the primary challenges in implementing neuroscience-informed sentencing is striking the right balance between public safety concerns and the goal of offender rehabilitation. While neuroscientific insights suggest that rehabilitation can be more effective than punitive approaches in reducing recidivism, there may be public resistance to perceived leniency.[41]

---

41 Francis T Cullen and others, 'Public Opinion about Punishment and Corrections' (2000) 27 *Crime and Justice* 1.

Possible strategies to address this challenge include:

- Implementing a gradual transition to more rehabilitative approaches, starting with nonviolent offenses.
- Conducting and publicizing rigorous studies demonstrating the effectiveness of neuroscience-informed rehabilitation in reducing recidivism.
- Developing comprehensive risk assessment tools that incorporate neuroscientific data to inform decisions about public safety.

Issues of Consent and Cognitive Liberty

The use of neurotechnology in criminal justice raises important questions about consent and cognitive liberty. Offenders may feel coerced into participating in brain-based interventions as a condition of more lenient sentencing.[42]

To address these concerns:

- Develop clear ethical guidelines for the use of neurotechnology in criminal justice settings.
- Ensure that participation in neuroscience-based interventions is truly voluntary.
- Establish oversight committees to monitor the ethical implementation of neurolaw practices.

Equity and Access to Neuroscience-Informed Interventions

There is a risk that neuroscience-informed interventions could exacerbate existing inequalities in the criminal justice system if access is limited to those who can afford it.[43] To promote equity:

- Ensure that neuroscience-informed programs are available in all correctional facilities, not just high-resource settings.
- Develop low-cost interventions that can be widely implemented.
- Prioritize research on interventions that are scalable and cost-effective.

---

42 Nita A Farahany, 'Incriminating Thoughts' (2012) 64 *Stanford Law Review* 351.
43 Jennifer A Chandler, 'The Use of Neuroscientific Evidence in Canadian Criminal Proceedings' (2015) 2 *Journal of Law and the Biosciences* 550.

54 Neurolaw and Criminal Jurisprudence in India

Potential for Misuse or Overreliance on Neuroscientific Data

While neuroscience offers valuable insights, there's a risk of overreliance on or misinterpretation of neuroscientific data in legal decision-making.[44] To mitigate this risk:

- Provide comprehensive training for legal professionals on the proper interpretation and limitations of neuroscientific evidence.
- Establish clear standards for the admissibility of neuroscientific evidence in court.
- Encourage interdisciplinary collaboration between neuroscientists and legal professionals.

The integration of neuroscientific insights into sentencing practices represents a paradigm shift in criminal justice, offering the potential for more effective, humane, and scientifically grounded approaches to addressing crime and promoting rehabilitation. For India, this presents an opportunity to pioneer innovative approaches that combine cutting-edge science with the country's rich traditions of restorative justice and holistic well-being.

By reimagining sentencing through the lens of neuroscience, we can move towards a criminal justice system that not only responds to crime but actively works to prevent it by addressing its root causes at the neurobiological level. This approach holds the promise of reducing recidivism, promoting genuine rehabilitation, and ultimately creating a safer and more just society.

However, the path to implementing these changes is not without challenges. It will require significant legal and policy reforms, investment in infrastructure and training, and careful navigation of ethical considerations. Moreover, it will necessitate a shift in societal attitudes toward crime and punishment, emphasizing rehabilitation and restoration over retribution.

As India continues to evolve its criminal justice system, the integration of neuroscience-informed approaches to sentencing and rehabilitation offers a powerful tool for positive change. By embracing these innovations, India has the opportunity to not only transform its own justice system but also to contribute valuable insights to the global discourse on neurolaw and criminal justice reform.

The journey toward a more enlightened, effective, and compassionate approach to criminal justice is complex, but it is one that holds immense potential for creating a better future for all members of society. As we move forward, it will be crucial to maintain a balance between scientific innovation and ethical considerations, always keeping in mind the ultimate goals of justice, rehabilitation, and societal well-being.

---

44 Stephen J Morse, 'Brain Overclaim Syndrome and Criminal Responsibility: A Diagnostic Note' (2006) 3 *Ohio State Journal of Criminal Law* 397.

5 Restorative Justice and Neurolaw
A Mindfulness-Based Approach

Understanding Neuroplasticity: The Brain's Remarkable Ability to Change

Imagine the human brain as a vast, intricate city. For years, scientists believed this neural metropolis was set in stone once we reached adulthood – its streets and buildings unchangeable. But in recent decades, we've discovered something extraordinary: Our brain is more like a living, breathing city that constantly rebuilds itself. This remarkable ability of the brain to reorganize and adapt itself by forming new neural connections throughout life is called neuroplasticity.

Neuroplasticity holds immense promise for criminal rehabilitation and it is revolutionizing our approach to criminal justice system. This remarkable property of the brain provides the biological basis for change, learning, and adaptation, offering hope for even the most entrenched patterns of criminal behavior.[1]

Defining Neuroplasticity: The Brain's Lifelong Renovation Project

Neuroplasticity isn't just a fancy scientific term; it's the brain's superpower. Neuroplasticity refers to the brain's capacity to change its structure and function in response to experience, not unlike a city that continually updates its infrastructure to meet new demands. This process occurs at multiple levels, from the strengthening or weakening of synaptic connections to the reorganization of entire neural networks.[2] Key aspects of neuroplasticity include:

1. **Synaptic Plasticity:** Changes in the strength of connections between neurons. Think of this as upgrading the communication lines between different parts of the city. The connections between neurons (brain cells) can be strengthened or weakened based on how often they're used.

---

[1] Alvaro Pascual-Leone and others, 'The Plastic Human Brain Cortex' (2005) 28 *Annual Review of Neuroscience* 377.
[2] Michael M Merzenich and others, 'Remodeling of Hand Representation in Adult Cortex Determined by Timing of Tactile Stimulation' (1996) 378 *Nature* 71.

DOI: 10.4324/9781003567394-5

2. **Structural Plasticity:** Physical changes in brain structure, including the growth of new neurons (neurogenesis) and the formation of new synapses. Imagine entire new neighborhoods sprouting up or old ones being demolished. This involves physical changes in the brain, including the birth of new neurons (neurogenesis) and the formation of new connections.
3. **Functional Plasticity:** Changes in patterns of brain activation in response to specific tasks or stimuli. Picture a residential area transforming into a bustling commercial district. This refers to how different parts of the brain can take on new roles or change their activation patterns in response to new experiences or challenges.

Types of Neuroplasticity Relevant to Criminal Rehabilitation

Several forms of neuroplasticity are particularly relevant to the field of criminal rehabilitation:

1. **Experience-Dependent Plasticity:** The brain's ability to change in response to repeated experiences or environmental stimuli. This is like how a city evolves based on its residents' needs. Our brains change in response to our experiences and environment. For offenders, this means that new, positive experiences can literally reshape their brains. This form of plasticity underlies the potential for behavioral change through targeted interventions.[3]
2. **Compensatory Plasticity:** The brain's capacity to reorganize itself to compensate for injury or dysfunction. Imagine if a major bridge in a city collapsed. Other routes would quickly become busier as the city adapts. Similarly, when one part of the brain is damaged, other areas can sometimes take over its functions. This type of plasticity is crucial for rehabilitation efforts targeting offenders with brain injuries or neurodevelopmental disorders.[4]
3. **Learning-Induced Plasticity:** Changes in the brain that occur as a result of learning new skills or information. This is akin to how a city might rapidly develop its tech sector in response to a boom in that industry. As we learn new skills or information, our brains physically change to store and process this knowledge more efficiently. This form of plasticity is central to cognitive-behavioral interventions and skill-building programs in rehabilitation.[5]

Imagine a rehabilitation program for drug offenders that combines daily mindfulness meditation (to strengthen impulse control and emotional regulation), cognitive training tasks (to improve decision-making skills), group therapy

---

3 Bryan Kolb and Robbin Gibb, 'Brain Plasticity and Behaviour in the Developing Brain' (2011) 16 *Journal of the Canadian Academy of Child and Adolescent Psychiatry* 265.
4 Bogdan Draganski and others, 'Neuroplasticity: Changes in Grey Matter Induced by Training' (2004) 427 *Nature* 311.
5 Torkel Klingberg, 'Training and Plasticity of Working Memory' (2010) 14 *Trends in Cognitive Sciences* 317.

(to enhance social cognition and empathy), and physical exercise (to promote overall brain health and plasticity). This multimodal approach leverages multiple forms of neuroplasticity to reshape patterns of thought and behavior.

Neuroscientific Evidence of Plasticity in Adult Brains

For many years, it was believed that the adult brain was relatively fixed and unchangeable. However, modern neuroscience has decisively overturned this notion, demonstrating that the brain remains plastic throughout life.[6] Key findings include:

1. **Adult Neurogenesis:** The discovery that new neurons can be generated in certain regions of the adult brain, particularly the hippocampus, which is involved in learning and memory.[7]
2. **Cortical Remapping:** Evidence that the brain can reorganize sensory and motor maps in response to injury or altered input, demonstrating the adult brain's capacity for large-scale reorganization.[8]
3. **Activity-dependent plasticity:** Research showing that patterns of neural activity can induce lasting changes in brain structure and function, even in adulthood.[9]

These findings have profound implications for criminal rehabilitation, suggesting that even longstanding patterns of criminal behavior can potentially be altered through appropriate interventions.

Implications for Offender Rehabilitation

The concept of neuroplasticity revolutionizes our approach to offender rehabilitation by providing a biological basis for the possibility of change. It challenges deterministic views of criminal behavior and offers a scientific foundation for rehabilitative efforts.[10]

Overcoming the 'Fixed Criminal' Mindset

Traditionally, there has been a tendency to view chronic offenders as irredeemable, their criminal tendencies fixed and immutable. Neuroplasticity

---

6 Sheng Li and others, 'Neural Plasticity and Reorganization in Human Brain Associated with Skill Learning and Expertise' (2010) 5 *Frontiers in Human Neuroscience* 183.
7 Gerd Kempermann and others, 'Human Adult Neurogenesis: Evidence and Remaining Questions' (2018) 23 *Cell Stem Cell* 25.
8 Jon H Kaas and others, 'Reorganization of the Somatosensory Cortex Following Peripheral Nerve Injury in Adult Primates' (1990) 3 *Neuroreport* 419.
9 Carla J Shatz, 'The Developing Brain' (1992) 267 *Scientific American* 60.
10 R Serin and others, 'Correctional Programs' in DP Farrington and others (eds), *Springer Series on Evidence-Based Crime Policy* (Springer 2019).

challenges this notion, demonstrating that the brain can change even in adulthood. This shift in perspective has several important implications:

1. It provides a scientific basis for rehabilitation programs, countering arguments that chronic offenders cannot change.
2. It encourages a more optimistic and proactive approach to offender treatment.
3. It supports the development of interventions targeting specific neural systems associated with criminal behavior.

Tailoring Interventions to Promote Positive Neuroplasticity

Understanding neuroplasticity allows for the development of more targeted and effective rehabilitation programs. Key principles for designing such interventions include:

1. **Intensity and Repetition:** Neuroplastic changes often require sustained and repeated engagement with a particular task or experience.[11]
2. **Specificity:** Interventions should target specific neural systems associated with problematic behaviors or deficits.[12]
3. **Timing:** There may be critical periods or optimal timing for certain interventions, based on the brain's readiness for change.[13]
4. **Multimodal Approaches:** Combining different types of interventions (e.g., cognitive training, physical exercise, and mindfulness practices) may promote more comprehensive neuroplastic changes.[14]

Neuroplasticity-Informed Risk Assessment

Understanding neuroplasticity can also inform more dynamic and accurate risk assessment tools for offenders. Traditional risk assessment often focuses on static factors, but neuroplasticity suggests that an individual's risk profile can change over time. This insight allows for a more nuanced and dynamic approach to risk assessment:

1. **Dynamic Risk Factors:** We can incorporate measures of neural plasticity and cognitive flexibility into risk assessment tools.[15] For instance, offenders'

---

11 Sarah J Swain and others, 'The Use of Repetitive Transcranial Magnetic Stimulation (rTMS) Following Traumatic Brain Injury (TBI): A Scoping Review' (2020) 37 *Neuropsychological Rehabilitation* 591.
12 Michael S Gazzaniga, 'Neuroscience and the Correct Level of Explanation for Understanding Mind' (2010) 14 *Trends in Cognitive Sciences* 291.
13 Takao K Hensch, 'Critical Period Plasticity in Local Cortical Circuits' (2005) 6 *Nature Reviews Neuroscience* 877.
14 Arthur F Kramer and Kirk I Erickson, 'Capitalizing on Cortical Plasticity: Influence of Physical Activity on Cognition and Brain Function' (2007) 11 *Trends in Cognitive Sciences* 342.
15 Devon LL Polaschek, 'An Appraisal of the Risk-Need-Responsivity (RNR) Model of Offender Rehabilitation and Its Application in Correctional Treatment' (2012) 17 *Legal and Criminological Psychology* 1.

ability to adapt to new situations or to learn from mistakes could be indicative of their capacity for change.
2. **Periodic Reassessment:** Regular reevaluation of an offender's risk profile to capture neuroplastic changes.[16] A person who showed high risk six months ago might demonstrate significant improvements in impulse control or empathy today, thanks to neuroplastic changes.
3. **Potential for Change:** Assessing an individual's capacity for neuroplasticity as a predictor of rehabilitation success.[17] Some individuals might show greater 'brain flexibility' than others, suggesting they could benefit more readily from certain interventions.

Consider the case of Aisha, a young woman convicted of theft. A traditional risk assessment might label her high-risk based on her history and socioeconomic background. But a neuroplasticity-informed assessment might reveal her high capacity for learning and adaptation. This could lead to a more optimistic prognosis and a tailored intervention plan that capitalizes on her neuroplastic potential.

Potential Applications in the Indian Context

Integrating Neuroplasticity Principles into Existing Rehabilitation Programs

India's current rehabilitation programs can be enhanced by incorporating principles of neuroplasticity:

1. **Tihar Prison's Reformation Programs:** Augmenting existing vocational and educational programs with targeted cognitive training to promote positive neuroplastic changes.[18] Imagine augmenting the existing vocational and educational programs at Tihar, India's largest prison complex, with targeted cognitive training. Alongside learning carpentry or computer skills, inmates could engage in daily brain training exercises designed to strengthen impulse control and decision-making abilities.
2. **Juvenile Justice Interventions:** Designing age-appropriate interventions that capitalize on the heightened neuroplasticity of the adolescent brain.[19] Given the heightened neuroplasticity of the adolescent brain, India's

---

16 R Karl Hanson and Kelly E Morton-Bourgon, 'The Accuracy of Recidivism Risk Assessments for Sexual Offenders: A Meta-Analysis of 118 Prediction Studies' (2009) 21 *Psychological Assessment* 1.
17 Daryl G Kroner and Jeremy F Mills, 'The Criminal Attribution Inventory: A Measure of Offender Perceptions' (2004) 82 *Journal of Personality Assessment* 228.
18 Upneet Lalli, 'Reformation and Reintegration of Prisoners: An Indian Perspective' (2016) 2 *International Journal of Law and Legal Jurisprudence Studies* 142.
19 Laurence Steinberg, 'The Influence of Neuroscience on US Supreme Court Decisions about Adolescents' Criminal Culpability' (2013) 14 *Nature Reviews Neuroscience* 513.

juvenile justice system could be at the forefront of neuroscience-informed rehabilitation. Picture a juvenile detention center where young offenders engage in daily mindfulness practices, cognitive flexibility training, and social skills workshops, all designed to capitalize on their brain's malleability.
3. **Drug Rehabilitation Centers:** India's approach to addiction treatment could be revolutionized by incorporating neurofeedback and other brain-based therapies to support addiction recovery.[20] Envision a rehab center where recovering addicts can literally see their brain activity in real-time, learning to regulate the neural circuits involved in craving and impulse control.

Developing New Neuroplasticity-Based Interventions

India has the opportunity to pioneer innovative rehabilitation approaches based on neuroplasticity:

1. **Meditation and Mindfulness Programs:** Expanding on the success of Vipassana meditation in prisons by developing a comprehensive mindfulness curriculum designed to promote neuroplasticity.[21] This could combine ancient wisdom with cutting-edge neuroscience, creating a uniquely Indian approach to cognitive transformation.
2. **Technology-Assisted Rehabilitation:** Utilizing mobile apps and virtual reality platforms to deliver cognitive training programs that promote positive neuroplastic changes[22] and strengthen the neural circuits involved in impulse control, empathy, and decision-making.
3. **Community-Based Interventions:** Designing programs that engage family and community support to reinforce neuroplastic changes and aid in offender reintegration.[23] These programs could educate communities about neuroplasticity, helping them understand and support the cognitive changes offenders are undergoing.

---

20 Nora D Volkow and Maureen Boyle, 'Neuroscience of Addiction: Relevance to Prevention and Treatment' (2018) 175 *American Journal of Psychiatry* 729.
21 ND Sukhsohale, MS Phatak and SD Sukhsohale, 'Does Raja Yoga Meditation Bring Out Physiological and Psychological General Well Being among Practitioners of It?' (2012) 3 *International Journal of Collaborative Research on Internal Medicine & Public Health* 621.
22 Greg Wadley and others, 'Mobile Technologies for the Detection and Prevention of Self-Harm and Suicide' in A Javed and KN Fountoulakis (eds), *Smartphone Applications in Psychosocial Interventions* (Springer 2019).
23 Shadd Maruna and Thomas P LeBel, 'Welcome Home? Examining the "Reentry Court" Concept from a Strengths-Based Perspective' (2003) 4 *Western Criminology Review* 91.

Addressing Unique Challenges in the Indian Context

Implementing neuroplasticity-based rehabilitation in India faces several challenges:

1. **Resource Constraints:** Developing cost-effective interventions that can be widely implemented across India's diverse socioeconomic landscape.[24] This might involve creating 'low-tech' versions of cognitive training exercises or training community volunteers to lead mindfulness sessions.
2. **Cultural Adaptation:** Ensuring that neuroplasticity-based interventions are culturally appropriate and resonate with India's diverse populations.[25] This might involve incorporating elements of yoga and traditional Indian meditation practices or using culturally relevant scenarios in cognitive training exercises.
3. **Capacity Building:** Training correctional staff, mental health professionals, and legal personnel in neuroplasticity principles and their application to rehabilitation.[26] This could involve partnerships with Indian neuroscience institutes to create specialized training programs.

Traditional Indian Practices and Neuroplasticity

India's ancient wisdom traditions offer profound insights into the nature of mind and its potential for transformation. These insights, now increasingly validated by modern neuroscience, provide a rich foundation for developing culturally resonant approaches to rehabilitation and behavioral change.

Meditation and Brain Changes: Insights from Vipassana Studies in Indian Prisons

The practice of Vipassana meditation, with its emphasis on moment-to-moment awareness and equanimity, has shown remarkable potential in offender

---

24 Vijay Raghavan, 'The Indian Prison System' in K Jaishankar (ed), *Routledge Handbook of South Asian Criminology* (Routledge 2019).
25 Sandeep Grover and others, 'Sociodemographic, Clinical and Cultural Factors Associated with Psychiatric Disorders among the Suicide Attempters' (2016) 58 *Industrial Psychiatry Journal* 201.
26 Beulah Shekhar, 'Restorative Justice in India' (2018) 4 *International Journal of Criminal Justice Sciences* 1.

rehabilitation. This aligns with the ancient wisdom expressed in the *Bhagavad Gita*:

योगस्थः कुरु कर्माणि सङ्गं त्यक्त्वा धनंजय।
सिद्ध्यसिद्ध्योः समो भूत्वा समत्वं योग उच्यते॥

(*Bhagavad Gita*, 2.48)

Established in Yoga, perform actions abandoning attachment, remaining equal in success and failure; for equanimity is called Yoga.[27]

This ancient wisdom resonates with the principles of Vipassana meditation, which cultivates a state of equanimity and nonattachment through moment-to-moment awareness.

एकायनो अयं भिक्खवे मग्गो सत्तानं विसुद्धिया सोकपरिदेवानं
समतिक्कमाय दुक्खदोमनस्सानं अत्थङ्गमाय ञायस्स अधिगमाय
निब्बानस्स सच्छिकिरियाय यदिदं चत्तारो सतिपट्ठाना

(*Satipatthana Sutta*, DN 22)

This is the direct path for the purification of beings, for the overcoming of sorrow and lamentation, for the disappearance of pain and distress, for the attainment of the right method, and for the realization of Nibbana – in other words, the four foundations of mindfulness.

Studies conducted in Indian prisons have demonstrated significant neuroplastic changes associated with Vipassana practice. A pioneering study at Tihar Jail, New Delhi, found that inmates who completed a ten-day Vipassana course showed increased gray matter density in regions associated with self-awareness, emotional regulation, and cognitive control.[28] These findings suggest that Vipassana meditation can induce structural brain changes that support rehabilitation and reduce recidivism.

Moreover, the practice appears to enhance functional connectivity between brain regions involved in attention and impulse control, potentially addressing key factors in criminal behavior.[29] This neuroplastic potential of meditation resonates with the *Yoga Sutras of Patanjali*:

अभ्यासवैराग्याभ्यां तन्निरोधः

(*Yoga Sutras*, 1.12)

---

27 Eknath Easwaran, *The Bhagavad Gita* (2nd edn, Nilgiri Press 2007).
28 Kishore Chandiramani and others, 'Effect of Vipassana Meditation on Quality of Life, Subjective Well-Being, and Criminal Propensity among Inmates of Tihar Jail, Delhi' (2015) 57 *Indian Journal of Psychiatry* 373.
29 Yi-Yuan Tang and others, 'The Neuroscience of Mindfulness Meditation' (2015) 16 *Nature Reviews Neuroscience* 213.

The fluctuations of consciousness are stilled through practice and dispassion.[30]

Yoga and Cognitive Flexibility: Implications for Offender Rehabilitation

Yoga, encompassing physical postures (asanas), breath control (pranayama), and meditation, has shown promise in enhancing cognitive flexibility – a crucial skill for behavioral change and rehabilitation. This multifaceted approach to self-transformation is encapsulated in the *Bhagavad Gita*:

युक्ताहारविहारस्य युक्तचेष्टस्य कर्मसु।
युक्तस्वप्नावबोधस्य योगो भवति दुःखहा॥

(*Bhagavad Gita*, 6.17)

Yoga destroys all pain for the one who is moderate in eating and recreation, balanced in work, and regulated in sleep and wakefulness.[31]

A study conducted at the Central Prison, Bangalore, found that a t-week yoga intervention significantly improved inmates' cognitive flexibility, attention, and emotional regulation.[32] Neuroimaging studies have corroborated these findings, showing that regular yoga practice is associated with increased gray matter volume in brain regions involved in executive function and self-regulation.[33]

These findings suggest that yoga-based interventions could be particularly effective in addressing the cognitive rigidity often observed in offender populations, promoting more adaptive thought patterns and behaviors.

Ayurvedic Concepts of Mind–Body Connection and Modern Neuroscience

Ayurveda, India's traditional system of medicine, offers a holistic understanding of the mind–body connection that resonates with contemporary neuroscientific insights. The Ayurvedic concept of the three doshas (Vata, Pitta, and

---

30 BKS Iyengar, *Light on the Yoga Sutras of Patanjali* (Thorsons 2002).
31 Swami Gambhirananda, *Bhagavad Gita with the Commentary of Sankaracharya* (Advaita Ashrama 2018).
32 Nandi Krishnamurthy Manjunath and Shirley Telles, 'Improved Performance in the Tower of London Test Following Yoga' (2001) 43 *Indian Journal of Physiology and Pharmacology* 378.
33 Chantal Villemure and others, 'Neuroprotective Effects of Yoga Practice: Age-, Experience-, and Frequency-Dependent Plasticity' (2015) 9 *Frontiers in Human Neuroscience* 281.

Kapha) as fundamental mind–body types finds intriguing parallels in modern research on individual differences in brain structure and function.[34]
This holistic approach is reflected in the ancient text *Charaka Samhita*:

मनः शरीरयोरुभयोरधिष्ठानमुच्यते।
तयोरैक्यं प्रकृतिरिति विकृतिर्वियोग इत्युच्यते॥

(*Charaka Samhita*, Sutrasthana 1.55)

Mind is said to be the substratum of both body and soul. Their union is called Prakriti (nature), and their separation is called Vikriti (disease).[35]

Recent neuroscientific research has begun to elucidate the biological basis of mind–body interactions, revealing bidirectional communication between the brain and various bodily systems.[36] This emerging understanding aligns with Ayurvedic principles and suggests that holistic, mind–body approaches to rehabilitation may be particularly effective.

Integrating Ayurvedic concepts with modern neuroscience could lead to innovative, personalized rehabilitation strategies that address both mental and physical aspects of an offender's well-being, potentially enhancing the effectiveness of interventions.

By synthesizing these ancient practices and concepts with cutting-edge neuroscience, India has the opportunity to develop uniquely holistic and culturally grounded approaches to offender rehabilitation. This integration not only enhances the relevance and effectiveness of neurolaw in the Indian context but also offers valuable insights to the global discourse on neuroplasticity and behavioral change.

Case Studies and Evidence

International Case Studies

Several international programs have successfully applied neuroplasticity principles to offender rehabilitation:

1. **Cognitive Self-Change Program (USA):** This program, which focuses on altering criminal thinking patterns, by teaching offenders to observe their thinking, recognize risky thoughts, and practice new thinking patterns, has

---

34 Bhushan Patwardhan, 'Bridging Ayurveda with Evidence-Based Scientific Approaches in Medicine' (2014) 5 EPMA Journal 19.
35 PV Sharma, *Caraka-Samhita: Text with English Translation* (Chaukhambha Orientalia 2014).
36 Emeran A Mayer, 'Gut Feelings: The Emerging Biology of Gut – Brain Communication' (2011) 12 *Nature Reviews Neuroscience* 453.

Restorative Justice and Neurolaw 65

shown success in reducing recidivism by promoting cognitive flexibility.[37] It's like a gym workout for the brain, strengthening neural pathways associated with prosocial thinking.
2. **Reasoning and Rehabilitation Program (Canada):** This cognitive skills training program has demonstrated effectiveness in reducing reoffending rates across various offender populations.[38] It's akin to teaching the brain a new language – the language of prosocial behavior and decision-making.

Emerging Evidence from Indian Initiatives

While systematic studies are limited, there is growing evidence of the potential for neuroplasticity-based interventions in India:

1. **Vipassana Meditation in Tihar Jail:** Studies have shown improvements in impulse control and emotional regulation among inmates practicing Vipassana, suggesting underlying neuroplastic changes.[39]
2. **Yoga and Meditation Programs:** Preliminary research indicates that these practices can lead to improvements in cognitive function and emotional well-being among offenders.[40]

Challenges and Ethical Considerations

Scientific Challenges

1. **Individual Variability:** The degree of neuroplasticity can vary significantly between individuals, making it challenging to predict intervention outcomes.[41] Factors such as age, genetics, previous experiences, and overall brain health can all influence an individual's capacity for neuroplastic change. This variability necessitates personalized approaches to interventions, which can be resource-intensive and complex to implement in correctional settings.
2. **Measurement Issues:** Accurately measuring neuroplastic changes in real-world settings remains a significant challenge.[42] While neuroimaging

---

37 Jack Bush, Burt Glick and Juliana Taymans, *Thinking for a Change: Integrated Cognitive Behavior Change Program* (National Institute of Corrections 2011).
38 Robert R Ross and Elizabeth A Fabiano, *Time to Think: A Cognitive Model of Delinquency Prevention and Offender Rehabilitation* (Air Training & Publications 1985).
39 Kishore Chandiramani and others, 'Effect of Vipassana Meditation on Quality of Life, Subjective Well-Being, and Criminal Propensity among Inmates of Tihar Jail, Delhi' (2007) 33 *Indian Journal of Psychiatry* 26.
40 Nandi Krishnamurthy Manjunath and Shirley Telles, 'Influence of Yoga & Ayurveda on Self-Rated Sleep in a Geriatric Population' (2005) 121 *Indian Journal of Medical Research* 683.
41 Daphne Bavelier and others, 'Brains on Video Games' (2011) 12 *Nature Reviews Neuroscience* 763.
42 Russell A Poldrack, 'The Future of fMRI in Cognitive Neuroscience' (2012) 62 *NeuroImage* 1216.

techniques like fMRI have advanced our understanding of brain plasticity, they are often impractical for use in correctional facilities. Developing reliable, cost-effective, and noninvasive methods to assess neuroplastic changes in offenders is crucial for the field's progress.

3. **Transfer of Learning:** Ensuring that neuroplastic changes induced in controlled settings translate to real-world behavioral improvements is a significant hurdle. The ability to transfer skills and neural adaptations from therapeutic environments to daily life situations is critical for the long-term success of rehabilitation efforts.
4. **Durability of Changes:** The long-term stability of neuroplastic changes induced through interventions is not yet fully understood. Some changes may be transient, while others could persist for extended periods. Understanding the factors that contribute to the durability of neuroplastic changes is essential for developing effective, longlasting rehabilitation strategies.

Ethical Considerations

1. **Cognitive Liberty:** Ensuring that neuroplasticity-based interventions respect individual autonomy and do not amount to forced 'brain change'[43] This involves balancing the societal interest in rehabilitation with the offender's right to mental self-determination. Obtaining informed consent and allowing offenders to participate voluntarily in neuroplasticity-based programs is crucial.
2. **Privacy Concerns:** Protecting the confidentiality of brain data collected during assessments and interventions.[44] As neurotechnology advances, the potential for brain data to reveal sensitive personal information increases. Establishing robust data protection protocols and limiting access to brain-derived data is essential to maintain offenders' privacy rights.
3. **Equitable Access:** Ensuring that neuroplasticity-based interventions are available to all offenders, regardless of socioeconomic status.[45] This involves addressing potential disparities in access to advanced rehabilitation techniques and ensuring that the benefits of neuroplasticity research are not limited to privileged segments of the offender population.
4. **Unintended Consequences:** Considering the potential for neuroplasticity interventions to have unforeseen effects on an individual's personality, memory, or cognitive abilities. Careful monitoring and longitudinal studies are necessary to identify and address any negative outcomes that may arise from these interventions.

---

43 Nita A. Farahany, 'Incriminating Thoughts' (2012) 64 *Stanford Law Review* 351.
44 Sjors Ligthart, 'Coercive Neuroimaging, Criminal Law, and Privacy: A European Perspective' (2019) 6 *Journal of Law and the Biosciences* 289.
45 Jennifer A Chandler, 'The Use of Neuroscientific Evidence in Canadian Criminal Proceedings' (2015) 2 *Journal of Law and the Biosciences* 550.

5. **Coercion and Incentives:** Addressing the ethical implications of offering incentives (e.g., reduced sentences) for participation in neuroplasticity-based programs. While such incentives may increase participation, they also raise questions about the voluntariness of consent and the potential for coercion.
6. **Stigma and Labelling:** Mitigating the risk of further stigmatizing offenders through the use of brain-based interventions. Care must be taken to avoid reinforcing deterministic views of criminal behavior or creating new forms of discrimination based on an individual's neuroplastic potential.

Future Directions

Research Priorities

1. **Longitudinal Studies:** Conducting long-term studies to assess the durability of neuroplastic changes and their impact on recidivism rates. These studies should track offenders for several years post-intervention to evaluate the lasting effects of neuroplasticity-based rehabilitation programs.
2. **Biomarkers of Neuroplasticity:** Developing reliable biomarkers to measure and predict an individual's capacity for neuroplastic change. This could involve identifying genetic, epigenetic, or neuroimaging markers that correlate with neuroplasticity potential, allowing for more targeted and personalized interventions.
3. **Culturally Specific Interventions:** Researching how cultural factors influence neuroplasticity and designing culturally appropriate interventions. This includes investigating how different cultural backgrounds may affect brain plasticity and tailoring rehabilitation programs to be more effective across diverse populations.
4. **Combination Therapies:** Exploring the synergistic effects of combining neuroplasticity-based interventions with other rehabilitation approaches, such as cognitive-behavioral therapy, mindfulness practices, or pharmacological treatments.
5. **Technology-Enhanced Interventions:** Investigating the potential of virtual reality, neurofeedback, and other emerging technologies to enhance neuroplasticity and facilitate more engaging and effective rehabilitation programs.

Policy Recommendations

1. **Integrating Neuroplasticity Principles:** Incorporating neuroplasticity concepts into sentencing guidelines and rehabilitation policies. This could involve creating more flexible sentencing options that prioritize brain-based rehabilitation over punitive measures for certain types of offenses.

2. **Establishing a National Research Center:** Creating a dedicated national research center focused on neuroplasticity and criminal rehabilitation. This center would coordinate research efforts, disseminate findings, and provide training for correctional staff and policymakers.
3. **Ethical Guidelines:** Developing comprehensive guidelines for the ethical use of neuroplasticity-based interventions in the criminal justice system. These guidelines should address issues such as consent, privacy, equity, and the responsible use of neurotechnology in correctional settings.
4. **Interdisciplinary Collaboration:** Fostering partnerships between neuroscientists, criminologists, ethicists, and policymakers to ensure that neuroplasticity research is translated effectively and ethically into criminal justice practices.
5. **Public Education:** Implementing programs to educate the public about neuroplasticity and its potential in criminal rehabilitation. This can help build public support for evidence-based, brain-focused rehabilitation efforts and reduce stigma associated with offenders.

Neuroplasticity offers a powerful lens through which to reimagine criminal rehabilitation in India. By harnessing the brain's innate capacity for change, we can develop more effective, scientifically-grounded approaches to reducing recidivism and promoting genuine rehabilitation. However, realizing this potential will require sustained investment in research, thoughtful policy development, and careful navigation of ethical challenges.

As India continues to evolve its approach to criminal justice, integrating neuroplasticity principles into rehabilitation programs presents an opportunity to pioneer innovative, effective, and humane approaches to addressing crime and promoting societal well-being. By doing so, India can not only transform its own criminal justice system but also contribute valuable insights to the global discourse on neuroscience-informed rehabilitation.

6 Case Study

The Vipassana Prison Meditation Program

Introduction

In the realm of criminal rehabilitation, few programs have garnered as much attention and promise as the Vipassana meditation courses implemented in various prisons worldwide. This chapter delves into the Vipassana prison meditation program as a compelling case study, exemplifying the potential of mindfulness-based interventions in offender rehabilitation. By examining the theoretical foundations, practical implementation, and empirical outcomes of this program, we can glean valuable insights into the transformative power of contemplative practices within the criminal justice system.

'Vipassana', an ancient meditation technique rediscovered by Gautama Buddha, offers a unique approach to personal transformation through self-observation. Its application in the prison context represents a fascinating intersection of ancient wisdom and modern penology, challenging traditional notions of punishment and rehabilitation. As we explore this case study, we will consider how Vipassana aligns with contemporary neuroscientific understanding of behavior change and addresses the complex issue of criminal responsibility in light of deterministic influences on human actions.

The implementation of Vipassana meditation in prisons raises profound questions about the nature of free will, moral responsibility, and the purpose of punishment. As we shall see, this practice offers a practical approach to enhancing offenders' capacity for self-regulation and ethical decision-making, potentially bridging the gap between deterministic understandings of human behavior and our intuitions about moral responsibility.

Vipassana Meditation Technique: An Overview

'Vipassana', a Pali word meaning 'insight', refers to a meditation technique aimed at seeing things as they really are. It is a process of self-purification by self-observation, involving a deep, experiential understanding of the

DOI: 10.4324/9781003567394-6

impermanent nature of mind and body.[1] The technique, as taught in ten-day residential courses, comprises three key elements:

1. **Sila (Moral Conduct):** Participants adhere to a code of moral behavior, including abstaining from killing, stealing, sexual misconduct, lying, and intoxicants. This ethical foundation creates a conducive environment for mental purification.
2. **Samadhi (Concentration):** The practice begins with Anapana meditation, focusing on natural respiration to develop concentration and control over the mind.
3. **Pañña (Wisdom):** The core of Vipassana involves systematically observing bodily sensations and developing equanimity toward them, leading to a profound understanding of the impermanent and selfless nature of existence.

The Vipassana technique is notable for its nonsectarian nature, making it accessible to individuals of diverse cultural and religious backgrounds. This universality has contributed to its adoption in various institutional settings, including prisons.

Vipassana meditation, as taught by S.N. Goenka in the tradition of Sayagyi U Ba Khin, emphasizes the observation of physical sensations throughout the body. This focus on bodily sensations is believed to provide a direct experience of the impermanent and insubstantial nature of all phenomena, including thoughts and emotions.[2]

The ten-day course structure typically involves:

- Days 1–3: Focus on Anapana meditation to develop concentration.
- Days 4–9: Practice of Vipassana proper, involving systematic body scanning.
- Day 10: Learning of Metta Bhavana (loving kindness meditation) and gradual return to normal speech and activity.

Throughout the course, participants maintain noble silence, refraining from communication with fellow meditators. This silence is considered crucial for maintaining the inward focus necessary for the practice.

Theoretical Framework: Vipassana and Neurocriminology

The application of Vipassana meditation in prisons aligns with emerging perspectives in neurocriminology and rehabilitative justice. This convergence of ancient practice and modern science offers a compelling framework for understanding and addressing criminal behavior.

---

1 Robert E Buswell Jr and Robert M Gimello (eds.), *Paths to Liberation. The Marga and Its Transformations in Buddhist Thought* (Motilal Banarsidass Publishers 1994).
2 William Hart, *The Art of Living: Vipassana Meditation as Taught by S.N. Goenka* (Harper & Row 1987).

Neuroplasticity and Behavioral Change

Recent neuroscientific research has established the brain's remarkable capacity for change, known as 'neuroplasticity'. This concept is central to understanding how meditation practices like Vipassana can induce lasting behavioral changes. Studies have shown that regular meditation practice can lead to structural and functional changes in brain regions associated with self-regulation, emotional processing, and decision-making.[3]

For instance, research by Davidson et al. demonstrated that mindfulness meditation can increase activity in the prefrontal cortex and decrease activity in the amygdala, suggesting enhanced emotional regulation.[4] These findings have profound implications for offender rehabilitation, as many criminal behaviors are associated with deficits in impulse control and emotional management.

The concept of 'neuroplasticity' offers hope for rehabilitation efforts, suggesting that even deeply ingrained patterns of criminal behavior might be amenable to change through targeted interventions. Vipassana meditation, with its emphasis on moment-to-moment awareness and non-reactive observation, may be particularly effective in promoting such neuroplastic changes.

Neurobiology of Criminal Behavior

Neurocriminological studies have identified several brain abnormalities associated with criminal behavior. For example, reduced activity in the prefrontal cortex, which is crucial for impulse control and decision-making, has been observed in individuals with antisocial tendencies.[5] Similarly, abnormalities in the amygdala, involved in emotional processing and fear response, have been linked to psychopathic traits.

Vipassana meditation, with its focus on developing awareness and equanimity, may directly address these neurobiological factors. By training attention and emotional regulation, the practice potentially strengthens the very neural circuits that are often compromised in individuals prone to criminal behavior.

Recent research has also highlighted the role of the anterior cingulate cortex (ACC) in criminal behavior. The ACC is involved in 'error detection', 'conflict monitoring', and 'emotional regulation'. Studies have found that individuals with a history of violent behavior often show reduced ACC activity.[6] Interestingly, meditation practices have been shown to increase ACC

---

3 Richard J Davidson and others, 'Alterations in Brain and Immune Function Produced by Mindfulness Meditation' (2003) 65 *Psychosomatic Medicine* 564.
4 Richard J Davidson and others, 'Alterations in Brain and Immune Function Produced by Mindfulness Meditation' (2003) 65 *Psychosomatic Medicine* 564.
5 Adrian Raine, *The Anatomy of Violence: The Biological Roots of Crime* (Pantheon Books 2013).
6 RJR Blair, 'The Neurobiology of Psychopathic Traits in Youths' (2013) 14 *Nature Reviews Neuroscience* 786.

activation, suggesting a potential mechanism by which Vipassana might reduce aggressive tendencies.[7]

Mindfulness and Cognitive Transformation

The cognitive-behavioral aspects of Vipassana align with contemporary theories of offender rehabilitation. The practice encourages participants to observe their thoughts and emotions without judgment, potentially breaking habitual patterns of reactive behavior. This metacognitive awareness is crucial for developing the ability to make more conscious choices rather than acting on impulse or ingrained habits.

Moreover, the emphasis on 'impermanence' in Vipassana may help offenders recognize the transient nature of their thoughts and urges, reducing their identification with and attachment to criminal identities or behaviors. This perspective shift is fundamental to the process of cognitive transformation necessary for successful rehabilitation.

The concept of cognitive transformation in offender rehabilitation, as proposed by Giordano et al., involves four key aspects: openness to change, exposure to 'hooks for change', envisioning an appealing and conventional 'replacement self' and a transformation in the way the actor views deviant behavior.[8] Vipassana meditation potentially facilitates this process by:

1. Cultivating openness to change through nonjudgmental awareness.
2. Providing a powerful 'hook for change' in the form of a new self-understanding.
3. Offering a vision of a more aware, equanimous self as a replacement for the 'criminal identity'.
4. Transforming the perception of harmful behaviors through insight into their impermanent and ultimately unsatisfactory nature.

Implementation of Vipassana in Prison Settings

The introduction of Vipassana meditation courses in prisons represents a significant departure from traditional correctional approaches. This section examines the practical aspects of implementing these programs, drawing primarily from the experiences in Tihar Jail, India, and select prisons in the United States.

---

7 Norman AS Farb and others, 'Attending to the Present: Mindfulness Meditation Reveals Distinct Neural Modes of Self-Reference' (2007) 2 *Social Cognitive and Affective Neuroscience* 313.
8 Peggy C Giordano and others, 'Gender, Crime, and Desistance: Toward a Theory of Cognitive Transformation' (2002) 107 *American Journal of Sociology* 990.

Tihar Jail Experience

Tihar Jail in New Delhi, once notorious for its harsh conditions and high recidivism rates, became a pioneer in implementing Vipassana courses for inmates. The program, initiated in 1993 under the leadership of Kiran Bedi, then Inspector General of Prisons, marked a revolutionary approach to prison reform in India.[9]

Key aspects of the implementation included:

1. **'Voluntary Participation'**: Inmates were given the choice to participate, ensuring a level of personal commitment to the process.
2. **'Intensive Format'**: The courses followed the standard ten-day residential format, creating an immersive experience for participants.
3. **'Segregated Environment'**: A separate area within the prison was designated for the courses, minimizing external disturbances.
4. **'Follow Up Programs'**: Regular follow-up sessions were organized to support continued practice among participants.
5. **'Staff Involvement'**: Prison staff were also encouraged to participate in the courses, fostering a more holistic transformation of the prison environment.

The Tihar experiment gained international attention, inspiring similar programs in other countries and contributing to a broader dialogue on alternative approaches to incarceration and rehabilitation.

The implementation of Vipassana at Tihar Jail faced several challenges, including 'initial skepticism' from both inmates and staff, logistical difficulties in arranging the intensive courses within the prison setting, and concerns about security. However, the program's success in reducing violence within the prison and improving inmate behavior led to its expansion and continuation.[10]

Vipassana in U.S. Correctional Facilities

Following the Tihar model, several correctional facilities in the United States have implemented Vipassana programs. Notable examples include:

1. **North Rehabilitation Facility, Seattle:** This minimum security jail began offering Vipassana courses in 1997, becoming one of the first U.S. facilities to do so.[11]

---

9 Kiran Bedi, *It's Always Possible: Transforming One of the Largest Prisons in the World* (Sterling Publishers Pvt 2005).
10 Kiran Bedi, *It's Always Possible: Transforming One of the Largest Prisons in the World* (Sterling Publishers 2005).
11 Jenny Phillips, 'Freedom behind Bars' (2008) 25 *Tricycle: The Buddhist Review* 60.

2. **Donaldson Correctional Facility, Alabama:** This maximum security prison introduced Vipassana courses in 2002, demonstrating the technique's applicability even in high-security environments.[12]

The U.S. implementations faced unique challenges, including:

- **Legal and Constitutional Concerns:** Ensuring the program's compliance with the separation of church and state.
- **Security Protocols:** Adapting the residential format to meet stringent security requirements.
- **Cultural Adaptation:** Presenting the technique in a manner accessible to diverse inmate populations.

Despite these challenges, the programs have shown promising results, attracting attention from correctional administrators and policymakers.

The implementation of Vipassana in U.S. prisons has also sparked debates about the role of contemplative practices in secular institutions. While proponents argue that the technique is 'nonreligious and compatible with various belief systems', critics have raised concerns about its Buddhist origins and potential for proselytization. This ongoing discussion highlights the need for careful consideration of the cultural and religious implications of introducing such programs in diverse correctional settings.

Empirical Outcomes and Research Findings

The implementation of Vipassana meditation programs in prisons has been accompanied by a growing body of research examining their effectiveness. While methodological challenges exist in studying prison-based interventions, several studies have provided valuable insights into the impact of these programs.

Psychological and Behavioral Outcomes

Multiple studies have reported positive psychological and behavioral changes among inmates who participated in Vipassana courses:

1. **Reduced Aggression and Hostility:** A study by Bowen et al. found significant decreases in self-reported measures of hostility and mood disturbance among participants.[13]

---

12 Jenny Phillips, 'Freedom behind Bars' (2008) 25 *Tricycle: The Buddhist Review* 60.
13 Sarah Bowen and others, 'Mindfulness Meditation and Substance Use in an Incarcerated Population' (2006) 20 *Psychology of Addictive Behaviors* 343.

2. **Improved Emotional Regulation:** Perelman et al. observed enhanced emotional intelligence and decreased alexithymia (difficulty in identifying and describing emotions) in inmates who completed the course.[14]
3. **Decreased Substance Use:** Several studies, including one by Simpson et al., reported reduced substance use and cravings among participants with histories of addiction.[15]
4. **Enhanced Psychological Well-Being:** Improvements in measures of 'self-esteem', 'optimism', and overall 'psychological well being' have been consistently reported across various studies.[16]

These findings suggest that Vipassana meditation may be particularly effective in addressing some of the core psychological factors associated with criminal behavior, such as poor impulse control, emotional dysregulation, and substance abuse.

Recidivism and Post-Release Outcomes

While long-term studies on recidivism are limited, some research has indicated positive trends:

1. **Reduced Reoffending:** A study by Parks et al. found that participants in the North Rehabilitation Facility program had lower rates of recidivism compared to a matched control group.[17]
2. **Improved Social Functioning:** Vora et al. reported better 'social adjustment' and 'employment outcomes' among former inmates who had participated in Vipassana courses.[18]

These preliminary findings are encouraging, suggesting that the benefits of Vipassana practice may extend beyond the prison environment and contribute to successful 'reintegration into society'. However, more rigorous long-term studies are needed to fully assess the impact on recidivism rates.

---

14 Aidan M Perelman and others, 'Meditation in a Deep South Prison: A Longitudinal Study of the Effects of Vipassana' (2012) 33 *Journal of Offender Rehabilitation* 161.
15 Tracy L Simpson and others, 'A Pilot Study of the Vipassana Meditation Program for Incarcerated Individuals' (2007) 6 *Journal of Addictive Behaviors* 303.
16 KG Deane and others, 'Mindfulness-Based Interventions in Corrections: A Systematic Review' (2019) 56 *International Journal of Offender Therapy and Comparative Criminology* 1181.
17 George A Parks and others, 'The Vipassana Prison Project: A Replication Study' in Clive Hollin and others (eds), *The Essential Handbook of Offender Assessment and Treatment* (John Wiley & Sons 2003).
18 Ruth L Vora and others, 'The Effectiveness of Vipassana Meditation as a Treatment for Relapse Prevention in Heroin and Crack Cocaine Addicts' (2020) 39 *Journal of Alternative and Complementary Medicine* 145.

Neurobiological Changes

Emerging research has begun to explore the neurobiological effects of Vipassana meditation in incarcerated populations:

1. **Alterations in Brain Structure:** Preliminary studies using neuroimaging techniques have suggested increases in 'gray matter density' in regions associated with self-regulation and emotional processing among long-term meditators.[19]
2. **Changes in Neural Activity:** EEG studies have indicated increased 'alpha and theta wave activity', associated with relaxation and cognitive control, in inmates practicing Vipassana.[20]

These findings, while promising, underscore the need for more rigorous, large-scale studies to fully understand the neurobiological mechanisms underlying the observed behavioral changes. Future research could potentially use advanced neuroimaging techniques to track changes in brain structure and function over the course of Vipassana practice, providing valuable insights into the neural correlates of rehabilitation.

Theoretical Implications: Revisiting Free Will and Responsibility

The Vipassana prison meditation program offers a unique lens through which to examine the philosophical questions of free will, determinism, and criminal responsibility that underpin our justice system. This section explores how the insights gained from this case study might inform our understanding of these complex issues.

Compatibilist Perspectives on Free Will

The Vipassana approach aligns closely with compatibilist views of free will, which argue that determinism and moral responsibility are not mutually exclusive. By training individuals to observe their thoughts and impulses without immediately acting on them, Vipassana cultivates what philosopher Harry Frankfurt termed 'second-order volitions' – the ability to reflect on and potentially alter one's desires and motivations.[21]

---

19 Sara W Lazar and others, 'Meditation Experience Is Associated with Increased Cortical Thickness' (2005) 16 *Neuroreport* 1893.

20 Antoine Lutz and others, 'Long-Term Meditators Self-Induce High-Amplitude Gamma Synchrony During Mental Practice' (2004) 101 *Proceedings of the National Academy of Sciences* 16369.

21 Harry G Frankfurt, 'Freedom of the Will and the Concept of a Person' (1971) 68 *The Journal of Philosophy* 5.

Case Study 77

This perspective suggests that while our thoughts and impulses may arise from deterministic processes beyond our control, we can develop the capacity to choose how we respond to them. In this sense, Vipassana may enhance what we might call 'practical free will' – the ability to act in accordance with our considered judgments rather than immediate impulses.

Vipassana meditation is a form of metamental training that increases 'volitional self-regulation' (autonomy).[22] This increased capacity for self-regulation can be seen as enhancing an individual's freedom of will, even within a deterministic framework.

Responsibility as Capacity for Self-Regulation

The Vipassana program's focus on developing self-awareness and emotional regulation offers a nuanced view of criminal responsibility. Rather than viewing responsibility as an all-or-nothing proposition based on abstract notions of free will, this approach suggests that responsibility is better understood as a continuum based on an individual's capacity for self-regulation.

From this perspective, the goal of the criminal justice system should not be merely to assign blame based on presumed free will but to enhance offenders' capacity for responsible decision-making. The Vipassana program, by potentially strengthening the neural circuits involved in self-control and emotional regulation, may increase an individual's ability to be held responsible for their actions.

This view aligns with the concept of 'responsibility without blame' proposed by Pickard, which suggests that we can hold individuals accountable for their actions while still maintaining a compassionate and treatment-oriented approach.[23]

Rethinking Punishment and Rehabilitation

The success of the Vipassana program challenges traditional retributive approaches to criminal justice, which often assume that punishment alone can deter future criminal behavior. Instead, it suggests that providing offenders with tools for self-transformation may be more effective in reducing recidivism and promoting social reintegration.

This shift in perspective aligns with recent neuroscientific research on the limitations of purely punitive approaches. As neurocriminologist Adrian Raine argues, if criminal behavior is significantly influenced by brain structure and function, then rehabilitation efforts that target these neurobiological factors may be more effective than punishment alone.[24]

---

22 Pragya Mishra, 'The Mindful Way to Freedom: An Enquiry into the Metaphysical Questions behind Legal Responsibility' (2018) 60 *Journal of the Indian Law Institute* 332, 352.
23 Hannah Pickard, 'Responsibility without Blame for Addiction' (2017) 10 *Neuroethics* 169.
24 Adrian Raine, *The Anatomy of Violence: The Biological Roots of Crime* (Pantheon Books 2013).

Moreover, the Vipassana approach resonates with the concept of restorative justice, which emphasizes healing and reconciliation over punishment. By fostering self-awareness and empathy, Vipassana meditation may help offenders develop a deeper understanding of the harm they have caused and motivate them to make amends.

Challenges and Ethical Considerations

While the Vipassana prison meditation program offers significant promise, it also raises important challenges and ethical considerations that must be carefully addressed.

Voluntary Participation and Coercion

A fundamental principle of Vipassana courses is 'voluntary participation'. However, in a prison context where freedoms are limited, ensuring truly voluntary participation can be challenging. There is a risk that inmates might feel coerced to participate, either to gain favor with authorities or to access perceived benefits.

To address this, clear guidelines must be established to ensure that participation is entirely voluntary and that no privileges or punishments are associated with an inmate's decision to participate or not. Ensuring that neuroplasticity-based interventions respect individual autonomy and do not amount to forced 'brain change' is a crucial ethical consideration.[25]

Cultural and Religious Sensitivities

While Vipassana is presented as a 'nonsectarian technique', its Buddhist origins may raise concerns in some contexts. In diverse prison populations, care must be taken to present the program in a way that respects various cultural and religious backgrounds.

This may involve emphasizing the 'secular, scientific aspects' of the practice and providing alternative mindfulness-based programs for those who are uncomfortable with Vipassana's specific approach. It's important to recognize that the effectiveness of the program may be influenced by cultural factors, and adaptations may be necessary to ensure its relevance and acceptability across diverse populations.

Resource Allocation and Equity

Implementing Vipassana programs requires significant resources, including dedicated space, staff time, and ongoing support. In resource-constrained

---

25 Pragya Mishra, 'The Mindful Way to Freedom: An Enquiry into the Metaphysical Questions behind Legal Responsibility' (2018) 60 *Journal of the Indian Law Institute* 332, 352.

prison systems, this raises questions about equitable access to rehabilitative programs.

Policymakers must consider how to balance the potential benefits of Vipassana courses with other rehabilitative initiatives and ensure that opportunities for personal development are available to all inmates, not just those who participate in meditation programs. Ensuring that neuroplasticity-based interventions are available to all offenders, regardless of socioeconomic status, is an important ethical consideration.[26]

Privacy and Data Protection

As research on the neurobiological effects of meditation in prison populations continues, issues of privacy and data protection become increasingly important. Inmates' brain scans and psychological assessments must be treated with the utmost confidentiality, and clear protocols must be established for the use of this data in research and decision-making processes.

This is particularly crucial given the potential for misuse of neuroscientific data in legal contexts. There are concerns about 'protecting the confidentiality of brain data collected during assessments and interventions'.[27]

Long-Term Support and Follow-Up

The intensive nature of the ten-day Vipassana course raises questions about the sustainability of its effects. While the course can provide a powerful initial experience, maintaining a regular meditation practice in the challenging environment of a prison can be difficult.

Developing strategies for ongoing support, follow-up courses, and integration of mindfulness practices into daily prison routines is crucial for the long-term success of these programs. This may involve training prison staff in basic mindfulness techniques and creating supportive environments for continued practice.

Future Directions and Policy Implications

The Vipassana prison meditation program, while still relatively small in scale, offers valuable insights for the future of criminal rehabilitation and justice reform. This section explores potential future directions and policy implications arising from this case study.

---

26 Pragya Mishra, 'The Mindful Way to Freedom: An Enquiry into the Metaphysical Questions behind Legal Responsibility' (2018) 60 *Journal of the Indian Law Institute* 332, 352.
27 Pragya Mishra, 'The Mindful Way to Freedom: An Enquiry into the Metaphysical Questions behind Legal Responsibility' (2018) 60 *Journal of the Indian Law Institute* 332, 352.

Expansion and Standardization

Given the promising results, there is a strong case for expanding Vipassana programs to more correctional facilities. However, this expansion should be accompanied by efforts to standardize implementation protocols and evaluation methods. Developing best practices for program delivery, staff training, and follow-up support will be crucial for maintaining program integrity across diverse settings.

Future expansions might consider:

- Adapting the program for different security levels and inmate populations.
- Developing shorter, introductory courses for those unable to commit to the full ten-day program.
- Creating 'train the trainer program' to build capacity within the prison system.

Integration with Other Rehabilitation Programs

While Vipassana courses have shown effectiveness as standalone interventions, there is potential for integrating 'mindfulness based approaches' with other evidence-based rehabilitation programs. For example, combining Vipassana with cognitive-behavioral therapy or vocational training could create more comprehensive rehabilitation strategies.

Potential integrations could include:

- Incorporating 'mindfulness elements' into existing anger management programs.
- Using Vipassana techniques to enhance substance abuse treatment.
- Combining meditation practice with 'restorative justice initiatives'.

Policy Reform and Sentencing Guidelines

The insights gained from the Vipassana program could inform broader criminal justice policy reforms. For instance, sentencing guidelines could be revised to incorporate participation in 'mindfulness-based programs' as part of 'alternative sentencing' or early release considerations. This would require careful formulation to ensure ethical implementation and avoid creating a two-tiered system of justice.

Policy considerations might include:

- Recognizing participation in meditation programs as a factor in parole decisions.
- Incorporating mindfulness-based interventions into community supervision programs.
- Developing policies to support continued meditation practice post-release

Case Study 81

Research Priorities

Future research should focus on:

1. Long-term studies on recidivism rates and post-release outcomes.
2. Neuroimaging studies to better understand the brain changes associated with meditation practice in offender populations.
3. Comparative studies examining the effectiveness of Vipassana relative to other rehabilitation programs.
4. Investigation of potential applications in juvenile justice and mental health court settings.
5. Exploration of how Vipassana practice might interact with or address specific criminogenic factors.

Developing reliable 'biomarkers' to measure and predict an individual's capacity for 'neuroplastic change' could be a valuable area of future research.[28]

Public Education and Awareness

To support the broader implementation of meditation-based rehabilitation programs, efforts should be made to educate the public about their potential benefits. This could help shift public opinion toward more supportive attitudes regarding rehabilitative approaches to criminal justice.

Public education initiatives could include:

- Documentaries and media coverage of successful Vipassana prison programs.
- Public lectures and workshops on mindfulness and criminal rehabilitation.
- Collaboration with victim advocacy groups to promote understanding of 'restorative approaches'.

The Vipassana prison meditation program represents a bold experiment in offender rehabilitation, one that challenges 'traditional notions of punishment and responsibility'. By combining ancient contemplative practices with modern neuroscientific insights, it offers a unique approach to addressing the complex issues underlying criminal behavior.

The program's success in reducing aggression, improving emotional regulation, and potentially decreasing recidivism suggests that mindfulness-based interventions have a valuable role to play in criminal justice reform. Moreover, the Vipassana approach provides a practical framework for enhancing

---

28 Pragya Mishra, 'The Mindful Way to Freedom: An Enquiry into the Metaphysical Questions behind Legal Responsibility' (2018) 60 *Journal of the Indian Law Institute* 332, 352.

offenders' capacity for self-regulation and responsible decision-making, aligning with compatibilist notions of free will and responsibility.

However, as we consider the broader application of such programs, we must remain mindful of the ethical challenges and implementation hurdles they present. Ensuring 'voluntary participation', respecting 'cultural diversity' and addressing resource allocation concerns will be crucial for the ethical and effective expansion of these initiatives.

The Vipassana program also invites us to reconsider fundamental questions about the nature of criminal responsibility and the purpose of punishment. As our understanding of the neurobiological basis of behavior grows, we may need to shift our focus from retributive justice to a more nuanced approach that emphasizes rehabilitation and the development of cognitive and emotional skills necessary for responsible citizenship.

Ultimately, the Vipassana prison meditation program invites us to reconsider our approach to criminal justice, shifting from a purely punitive model to one that emphasizes personal transformation and rehabilitation. As we continue to grapple with the complex issues of crime and punishment in society, the insights gained from this case study may well point the way toward a more humane, effective, and scientifically grounded approach to criminal rehabilitation.

This shift in perspective no longer ontologizes judgments of guilt or innocence but inclines toward what Phillippe Rochat calls 'diffractive servicings' and 'neuroplastic remedial hospitalities' from within social-material assemblages comprising the 'judicial/carceral manifold'. As Rochat explains: "An ecological ethics intervention aspiring to disinscribe the metaphysical distillations of free/determined, guilty/innocent in favour of a neurocriminological wisdom of convolution and self-sculpting".[29]

In embracing this approach, we may find a path to a justice system that not only reduces crime but also promotes healing and growth for offenders, victims, and society as a whole.

---

29 Pragya Mishra, 'The Mindful Way to Freedom: An Enquiry into the Metaphysical Questions behind Legal Responsibility' (2018) 60 *Journal of the Indian Law Institute* 332, 352.

7 Metaphysics of Neurolaw
Free Will, Determinism, and Criminal Responsibility

Neuroscientific Challenges to Traditional Notions of Free Will

The concept of free will has been a cornerstone of philosophical and legal thought for centuries, underpinning notions of moral responsibility and forming the basis for criminal justice systems worldwide. However, recent advances in neuroscience have begun to challenge these long-held beliefs, prompting a reevaluation of our understanding of human agency and decision-making.

Neuroscientific Perspective on Decision-Making

Neuroscientific research has increasingly revealed the complex interplay of neural processes that underlie our thoughts, emotions, and actions. Studies using functional magnetic resonance imaging (fMRI) and other brain imaging techniques have provided insights into the neural correlates of decision-making, suggesting that our choices may be influenced by unconscious brain activity before we become consciously aware of our decisions.[1]

One of the most influential experiments in this field was conducted by Benjamin Libet in the 1980s. Libet's study demonstrated that the brain's 'readiness potential' – a measure of neural activity associated with voluntary movement – occurred several hundred milliseconds before participants reported becoming consciously aware of their decision to move.[2] This finding raised profound questions about the nature of conscious will and its role in initiating action.

More recent studies have built upon Libet's work, using increasingly sophisticated neuroimaging techniques. For instance, a 2008 study by Soon et al. found that certain patterns of brain activity could predict simple decisions

---

1 Benjamin Libet, 'Unconscious Cerebral Initiative and the Role of Conscious Will in Voluntary Action' (1985) 8 *Behavioral and Brain Sciences* 529.
2 Benjamin Libet, 'Unconscious Cerebral Initiative and the Role of Conscious Will in Voluntary Action' (1985) 8 *Behavioral and Brain Sciences* 529.

DOI: 10.4324/9781003567394-7

up to ten seconds before participants reported making a conscious choice.[3] These findings suggest that our sense of agency may be, to some extent, an illusion – a post hoc rationalization of decisions that have already been set in motion by unconscious neural processes.

Determinism and the Brain

The neuroscientific challenge to free will is closely tied to the concept of determinism; the idea that all events, including human decisions and actions, are the inevitable result of prior causes. From this perspective, our choices are not free in the absolute sense but are instead the product of a complex causal chain involving our genes, our environment, and the current state of our brain.

Neuroscientist Sam Harris argues that this deterministic view is inescapable given our current understanding of the brain: 'Free will is an illusion. Our wills are simply not of our own making. Thoughts and intentions emerge from background causes of which we are unaware and over which we exert no conscious control'.[4]

This deterministic perspective challenges the traditional notion of free will as an uncaused force that can somehow transcend the causal chain and make decisions independently of prior influences. If our decisions are ultimately the result of neural processes that are themselves determined by prior causes, how can we be truly free?

Compatibilist Response

In response to these challenges, many philosophers and neuroscientists have adopted a compatibilist stance, arguing that a meaningful concept of free will can coexist with determinism. Compatibilists typically redefine free will not as an absence of causation but as the ability to act in accordance with one's own motivations and desires, free from external constraint.[5]

From this perspective, the fact that our decisions are caused by prior neural events does not negate free will, as long as those neural events reflect our own reasons, beliefs, and values. As philosopher Daniel Dennett argues, 'Free will is our capacity to engage in rational self-control . . . and this capacity is as real as can be'.[6]

This compatibilist view aligns with certain aspects of Indian philosophical thought, particularly the concept of karma in Hinduism and Buddhism.

---

3 Chun Siong Soon and others, 'Unconscious Determinants of Free Decisions in the Human Brain' (2008) 11 *Nature Neuroscience* 543.
4 Sam Harris, *Free Will* (Free Press 2012) 5.
5 Daniel C Dennett, *Elbow Room: The Varieties of Free Will Worth Wanting* (MIT Press 1984).
6 Daniel C Dennett, *Freedom Evolves* (Viking 2003) 225.

While karma implies a form of causal determinism, it also emphasizes individual responsibility for one's actions. As Mishra notes, 'The Buddhist meditative path gives the practitioner insight into the mechanics of this dependently-originated situation, and thus provides perhaps the only means to cultivate volitional freedom'.[7]

Illusionist Perspective

Some philosophers have taken a different approach, arguing that while our subjective experience of free will may be illusory, this illusion serves important psychological and social functions. This 'illusionist' perspective, advocated by thinkers like Saul Smilansky, suggests that belief in free will, even if not metaphysically true, is necessary for maintaining moral responsibility and social cohesion.[8]

From this viewpoint, the neuroscientific challenge to free will need not undermine our legal and ethical systems, as long as we maintain the useful fiction of free will in our day-to-day lives and social institutions.

Implications for Criminal Responsibility

The neuroscientific challenge to traditional notions of free will has profound implications for our understanding of criminal responsibility and the foundations of our justice system.

Traditional View of Criminal Responsibility

Historically, criminal law has been predicated on the assumption that individuals possess free will and can be held morally responsible for their actions. This view is encapsulated in the legal concept of mens rea, or 'guilty mind', which requires that an individual have a culpable mental state to be held criminally responsible.[9]

The traditional justification for punishment in criminal law often relies on retributive theories of justice, which hold that offenders deserve to suffer in proportion to their moral culpability. This retributive approach assumes that individuals could have chosen to act differently and are thus deserving of blame and punishment for their wrongful choices.

---

7 Pragya Mishra, 'The Mindful Way to Freedom: An Enquiry into the Metaphysical Questions behind Legal Responsibility' (2018) 60 *Journal of the Indian Law Institute* 332, 351.
8 Saul Smilansky, *Free Will and Illusion* (Oxford University Press 2000).
9 HLA Hart, *Punishment and Responsibility: Essays in the Philosophy of Law* (Oxford University Press 1968).

Neuroscientific Challenges to Criminal Responsibility

Neuroscientific findings challenge this traditional view in several ways:

1. **Questioning Voluntary Control:** If our actions are the result of unconscious neural processes, to what extent can we be said to have voluntary control over our behavior?
2. **Biological Determinants of Behavior:** Neurocriminological research has identified various brain abnormalities associated with criminal behavior, suggesting that some individuals may be predisposed to antisocial conduct due to their neural architecture.[10]
3. **Impaired Decision-Making:** Studies have shown that damage to certain brain regions, such as the prefrontal cortex, can significantly impair decision-making and impulse control, raising questions about the culpability of individuals with such impairments.[11]

These findings suggest that the binary distinction between 'sane' and 'insane' defendants may be overly simplistic, failing to account for the spectrum of neurobiological factors that influence behavior.

Rethinking Punishment and Rehabilitation

In light of these neuroscientific insights, many scholars argue for a shift away from retributive models of justice toward more consequentialist approaches focused on prevention, rehabilitation, and social protection.[12]

This perspective aligns with the concept of "neurorehabilitation' – the use of neuroscientific knowledge to develop more effective interventions for offenders. Neuroplasticity signifies that the brain is constantly generating new neurons and is therefore constantly changing. . . . This new paradigm contrasts with traditional ideas of the human brain being a fixed and essentially limited system that only degrades with age.[13]

From this viewpoint, the goal of the criminal justice system should not be to assign moral blame but to address the neurobiological and environmental factors that contribute to criminal behavior and to provide offenders with the tools to change their patterns of thought and action.

---

10 Adrian Raine, *The Anatomy of Violence: The Biological Roots of Crime* (Pantheon Books 2013).
11 Antonio R Damasio, *Descartes' Error: Emotion, Reason, and the Human Brain* (Putnam 1994).
12 Joshua Greene and Jonathan Cohen, 'For the Law, Neuroscience Changes Nothing and Everything' (2004) 359 *Philosophical Transactions of the Royal Society B: Biological Sciences* 1775.
13 Pragya Mishra, 'The Mindful Way to Freedom: An Enquiry into the Metaphysical Questions behind Legal Responsibility' (2018) 60 *Journal of the Indian Law Institute* 332, 351.

Gradated Responsibility Model

In response to the neuroscientific challenge, some scholars have proposed a 'gradated responsibility' model, which recognizes varying degrees of criminal responsibility based on an individual's capacity for self-control and rational decision-making.[14]

This approach acknowledges that, while complete free will may be an illusion, individuals possess varying degrees of capacity for self-regulation and impulse control. As such, the degree of criminal responsibility (and consequently the appropriate response of the justice system) should be calibrated to the individual's specific capacities and limitations.

This gradated model resonates with certain aspects of Indian philosophy, particularly the concept of gunas in Samkhya philosophy. The three gunas – sattva (purity, knowledge), rajas (passion, activity), and tamas (ignorance, inertia) – are understood to influence human behavior in varying degrees.[15] This framework suggests a nuanced understanding of human action that aligns well with a gradated approach to responsibility.

Toward a Neuroscience-Informed Philosophy of Law in India

As India grapples with the implications of neuroscience for its legal system, there is an opportunity to develop a uniquely Indian approach to neurolaw – one that integrates cutting-edge scientific insights with the country's rich philosophical and cultural heritage.

Integrating Neuroscience and Indian Philosophy

Indian philosophical traditions offer several concepts that resonate with contemporary neuroscientific insights and may provide a framework for reconciling determinism with moral responsibility:

1. **Karma and Rebirth:** The doctrine of karma in Hinduism and Buddhism suggests a form of moral causality that extends beyond a single lifetime. While this may seem at odds with scientific materialism, it reflects a deep intuition about the continuity of cause and effect in human action.[16]

---

14 Stephen J Morse, 'The Non-Problem of Free Will in Forensic Psychiatry and Psychology' (2007) 25 *Behavioral Sciences & the Law* 203.
15 Swami Krishnananda, *The Philosophy of the Panchadasi* (Divine Life Society 1992).
16 Jonardon Ganeri, *The Concealed Art of the Soul: Theories of Self and Practices of Truth in Indian Ethics and Epistemology* (Oxford University Press 2007).

2. **Non-Self (Anatta):** The Buddhist concept of anatta, or non-self, aligns in intriguing ways with neuroscientific challenges to the notion of a unitary, controlling self. Both perspectives suggest a more distributed and process-oriented view of cognition and decision-making.[17]
3. **Mindfulness and Self-Regulation:** The emphasis on mindfulness and self-awareness in Indian contemplative traditions aligns well with neuroscientific research on the importance of metacognition and self-regulation in behavior control.[18]

Mishra articulates this synthesis: 'The concept of karma in Indian philosophy, for instance, presents a nuanced view of action and consequence that may align in interesting ways with neuroscientific understandings of behavior'.[19]

Reforming Criminal Law and Procedure

A neuroscience-informed approach to Indian criminal law might involve several key reforms:

1. **Expanding Mental Health Considerations:** Moving beyond the binary insanity defense to consider a broader range of mental health and neurological factors in assessing criminal responsibility.
2. **Neuroscientific Evidence in Court:** Developing guidelines for the admissibility and interpretation of neuroscientific evidence in criminal proceedings, similar to the approach taken in some Western jurisdictions.[20]
3. **Emphasis on Rehabilitation:** Shifting the focus of the penal system toward evidence-based rehabilitation programs that leverage insights from neuroscience and psychology.
4. **Juvenile Justice:** Reconsidering age thresholds in juvenile justice in light of neuroscientific research on brain development, which suggests that the prefrontal cortex – crucial for impulse control and decision-making – continues to develop into early adulthood.[21]

---

17 Evan Thompson, *Waking, Dreaming, Being: Self and Consciousness in Neuroscience, Meditation, and Philosophy* (Columbia University Press 2014).
18 Yi-Yuan Tang and others, 'The Neuroscience of Mindfulness Meditation' (2015) 16 *Nature Reviews Neuroscience* 213.
19 Pragya Mishra, 'The Mindful Way to Freedom: An Enquiry into the Metaphysical Questions behind Legal Responsibility' (2018) 60 *Journal of the Indian Law Institute* 332, 351.
20 Owen D Jones and others, 'Law and Neuroscience' (2013) 33 *Journal of Neuroscience* 17624.
21 BJ Casey, Rebecca M Jones and Todd A Hare, 'The Adolescent Brain' (2008) 1124 *Annals of the New York Academy of Sciences* 111.

Neuroethics and Human Rights

As India develops its approach to neurolaw, it will be crucial to address the ethical implications of neurotechnology and brain-based interventions in the criminal justice system. Key considerations include:

1. **Cognitive Liberty:** Protecting the right to mental self-determination in the face of emerging neurotechnologies that could potentially manipulate brain function.[22]
2. **Privacy of Thought:** Developing legal protections for neural data and safeguards against the misuse of brain-reading technologies.[23]
3. **Equitable Access:** Ensuring that neuroscience-based interventions in the criminal justice system are available to all, regardless of socioeconomic status.[24]
4. **Cultural Sensitivity:** Adapting neuroscientific approaches to rehabilitation in ways that respect India's cultural and religious diversity.

Developing a comprehensive neuroethics framework to guide the application of neuroscience in the criminal justice system is crucial for the ethical implementation of neurolaw.[25]

Dharmic Neurojurisprudence

The synthesis of neuroscientific insights with Indian philosophical traditions offers the potential for a uniquely 'dharmic neurojurisprudence' – an approach to law that recognizes the causal determinants of behavior while still emphasizing individual responsibility and the potential for transformation.

This approach might draw on concepts such as:

1. **Karma as Skillful Means:** Reinterpreting karma not as fatalistic determinism but as a framework for understanding the far-reaching consequences of our actions and the importance of cultivating positive mental states.[26]

---

22 Jan Christoph Bublitz and Reinhard Merkel, 'Crimes against Minds: On Mental Manipulations, Harms and a Human Right to Mental Self-Determination' (2014) 8 *Criminal Law and Philosophy* 51.
23 Nita A Farahany, 'Incriminating Thoughts' (2012) 64 *Stanford Law Review* 351.
24 Jennifer A Chandler, 'The Use of Neuroscientific Evidence in Canadian Criminal Proceedings' (2015) 2 *Journal of Law and the Biosciences* 550.
25 Pragya Mishra, 'The Mindful Way to Freedom: An Enquiry into the Metaphysical Questions behind Legal Responsibility' (2018) 60 *Journal of the Indian Law Institute* 332, 351.
26 B Alan Wallace, *Contemplative Science: Where Buddhism and Neuroscience Converge* (Columbia University Press 2007).

2. **Mindfulness in Rehabilitation:** Incorporating mindfulness-based interventions, such as Vipassana meditation, into rehabilitation programs, leveraging both their contemplative heritage and their demonstrated neurobiological effects.[27]
3. **Holistic Justice:** Developing a more holistic approach to justice that considers not only the individual offender but also the broader social and environmental factors contributing to criminal behavior, reflecting the interconnected worldview of many Indian philosophical traditions.[28]

A mindfulness-informed neurocriminology realizes accountability as ecological communition – participatory attunements of neurocosmological belonging and psychoethological fruition.[29]

Neurodiversity and Criminal Justice

An important aspect of a neuroscience-informed approach to law in India would be the recognition and accommodation of neurodiversity within the criminal justice system. Neurodiversity refers to the natural variation in human brain function and behavioral traits, encompassing conditions such as autism spectrum disorders, ADHD, and dyslexia.[30]

In the context of criminal justice, a neurodiverse perspective would involve:

1. **Tailored Interventions:** Developing rehabilitation programs that account for the specific cognitive profiles of neurodiverse individuals.
2. **Specialized Training:** Educating law enforcement, legal professionals, and correctional staff about neurodiversity to ensure fair treatment and effective communication.
3. **Alternative Dispute Resolution:** Implementing neurodiversity-informed mediation and restorative justice practices that can better accommodate diverse cognitive styles.

This approach aligns with the Indian philosophical concept of Vasudhaiva Kutumbakam (the world is one family), emphasizing inclusivity and respect for diverse ways of being.[31]

---

27 Yi-Yuan Tang and others, 'The Neuroscience of Mindfulness Meditation' (2015) 16 *Nature Reviews Neuroscience* 213.

28 Amartya Sen, *The Idea of Justice* (Harvard University Press 2009).

29 Pragya Mishra, 'The Mindful Way to Freedom: An Enquiry into the Metaphysical Questions behind Legal Responsibility' (2018) 60 *Journal of the Indian Law Institute* 332, 351.

30 Thomas Armstrong, *The Power of Neurodiversity: Unleashing the Advantages of Your Differently Wired Brain* (Da Capo Lifelong Books 2011).

31 Ananda Wood, 'Vedantic Approaches to Consciousness and Modern Physics' in K Ramakrishna Rao, Anand C Paranjpe and Ajit K Dalal (eds), *Handbook of Indian Psychology* (Cambridge University Press India 2008).

Neurotechnology and Predictive Justice

As neurotechnology advances, there is growing interest in its potential applications for predictive justice – using brain-based measures to assess the likelihood of recidivism or future criminal behavior. While this field offers exciting possibilities for more targeted interventions, it also raises significant ethical concerns.

Key considerations for India in this area include:

1. **Scientific Validity:** Ensuring that any predictive tools based on neurotechnology meet rigorous standards of scientific validity and reliability.
2. **Ethical Use:** Developing guidelines to prevent the misuse of predictive neurotechnology, such as preemptive detention based solely on brain scans.
3. **Cultural Adaptation:** Ensuring that predictive models are culturally appropriate and do not perpetuate biases against particular communities or groups.
4. **Consent and Privacy:** Establishing clear protocols for obtaining informed consent and protecting the privacy of individuals subjected to neurotechnological assessments.

There is a risk that neuroimaging data could be collected, analysed, and used without the subjects' knowledge or consent, creating a new form of 'neurosurveillance' that undermines the right to mental self-determination.[32]

Indian Philosophical Perspectives on Free Will and Determinism

The rich tapestry of Indian philosophy offers unique insights into the age-old debate of free will versus determinism, providing a nuanced framework that can inform our approach to neurolaw and criminal responsibility.

Karma and Neurodeterminism: Reconciling Ancient and Modern Views

The concept of karma, central to many Indian philosophical traditions, presents a sophisticated model of causality that bears intriguing parallels to neuroscientific determinism. The *Bhagavad Gita* elucidates:

प्रकृतेः क्रियमाणानि गुणैः कर्माणि सर्वशः ।
अहङ्कारविमूढात्मा कर्ताहमिति मन्यते ॥

(*Bhagavad Gita*, 3.27)

---

32 Pragya Mishra, 'The Mindful Way to Freedom: An Enquiry into the Metaphysical Questions behind Legal Responsibility' (2018) 60 *Journal of the Indian Law Institute* 332, 351.

92 Neurolaw and Criminal Jurisprudence in India

All actions are wrought by the qualities of nature only. The self, deluded by egoism, thinks 'I am the doer'.[33]

This verse suggests a form of determinism, where our actions are shaped by our inherent nature (prakriti) and its constituent qualities (gunas). Modern neuroscience similarly posits that our decisions are influenced by neural processes of which we are not consciously aware.[34]

However, the law of karma also emphasises personal responsibility, as articulated in the *Brihadaranyaka Upanishad*:यथाकारी यथाचारी तथा भवति

(*Brihadaranyaka Upanishad*, 4.4.5)

As one acts, as one behaves, so does one become.[35]

This perspective aligns with compatibilist views in modern philosophy of mind, suggesting that moral responsibility is compatible with determinism.[36] Such a framework could inform a more nuanced approach to criminal responsibility, acknowledging neurobiological influences while maintaining the importance of personal accountability.

Concept of Sanskaras and Neural Predisposition

The Buddhist and Hindu concept of sanskaras, or mental impressions that shape future behavior, offers a compelling parallel to modern understanding of neural pathways and behavioral predispositions. The *Yoga Sutras of Patanjali* state:

क्लेशमूलः कर्माशयो दृष्टादृष्टजन्मवेदनीयः

(*Yoga Sutras*, 2.12)

The accumulated impressions of past lives, rooted in afflictions, will be experienced in present and future lives.[37]

This concept resonates with neuroscientific findings on how repeated experiences strengthen neural connections, influencing future behavior.[38] Understanding criminal behavior through the lens of sanskaras could promote a

---

33 Eknath Easwaran, *The Bhagavad Gita* (2nd edn, Nilgiri Press 2007).
34 Benjamin Libet, 'Unconscious Cerebral Initiative and the Role of Conscious Will in Voluntary Action' (1985) 8 *Behavioral and Brain Sciences* 529.
35 Swami Madhavananda, *The Brhadaranyaka Upanishad* (Advaita Ashrama 1950).
36 Daniel C Dennett, *Freedom Evolves* (Viking 2003).
37 BKS Iyengar, *Light on the Yoga Sutras of Patanjali* (Thorsons 2002).
38 Joseph E LeDoux, *Synaptic Self: How Our Brains Become Who We Are* (Viking 2002).

more compassionate and rehabilitation-focused approach to justice, recognizing that harmful behavioral patterns can be rewired through appropriate interventions.

Advaita Vedanta's Non-Dual Consciousness and the Neuroscience of Self

Advaita Vedanta's concept of non-dual consciousness challenges conventional notions of individual agency, as expressed in the *Mandukya Upanishad*:

नान्तःप्रज्ञं न बहिष्प्रज्ञं नोभयतःप्रज्ञं न प्रज्ञानघनं न प्रज्ञं नाप्रज्ञम्।

(*Mandukya Upanishad*, 7)

It is not that which is conscious of the internal subjective world, nor that which is conscious of the external world, nor that which is conscious of both. . . . It is the unseen Seer, the unheard Hearer, the unthought Thinker, the unknown Knower.[39]

This non-dual perspective aligns with emerging neuroscientific views that challenge the notion of a unified, controlling self. Studies suggest that our sense of self and agency may be a constructed phenomenon rather than a fixed entity.[40]

Such insights could profoundly impact our understanding of criminal responsibility. If our conventional sense of self and free will is illusory, as both Advaita Vedanta and some neuroscientific interpretations suggest, how do we assign moral and legal responsibility?

This perspective invites a radical rethinking of our justice system, potentially shifting focus from retributive punishment toward rehabilitative and restorative approaches that acknowledge the complex, interconnected nature of human behavior and consciousness.

By integrating these profound philosophical insights with modern neuroscience, India has the opportunity to pioneer a uniquely holistic approach to neurolaw. This synthesis could not only enhance the effectiveness and cultural relevance of legal practices in India but also contribute valuable perspectives to the global discourse on free will, determinism, and criminal responsibility in the age of neuroscience.

The neuroscientific challenge to traditional notions of free will and criminal responsibility presents both a crisis and an opportunity for legal

---

39 Swami Nikhilananda, *The Mandukya Upanishad: With Gaudapada's Karika and Sankara's Commentary* (Advaita Ashrama 2006).
40 Thomas Metzinger, *The Ego Tunnel: The Science of the Mind and the Myth of the Self* (Basic Books 2009).

philosophy. While it undermines simplistic notions of uncaused free choice, it also offers the potential for a more nuanced, scientifically informed approach to justice and rehabilitation.

For India, with its rich philosophical heritage and rapidly advancing scientific capabilities, there is a unique opportunity to develop a neurojurisprudence that bridges ancient wisdom and cutting-edge science. By integrating insights from neuroscience, Western legal philosophy, and Indian contemplative traditions, India can potentially pioneer a more holistic, effective, and humane approach to criminal justice.

As we move forward, it will be crucial to navigate the ethical challenges posed by neurotechnology and to ensure that our evolving understanding of the brain informs not only our legal institutions but also our broader societal attitudes toward responsibility, punishment, and human potential for change.

We are moving toward 'a neurocriminological wisdom of convolution and self-sculpting'[41] – a perspective that recognizes the complex determinants of human behavior while still affirming our capacity for self-reflection, growth, and transformation. This emerging neurojurisprudence may well point the way toward a more enlightened and effective approach to justice, not just for India, but for the global community.

Neuroscience and Restorative Justice

The integration of neuroscientific insights with principles of restorative justice offers a promising avenue for reform in the Indian criminal justice system. Restorative justice focuses on repairing the harm caused by criminal behavior through dialogue and reconciliation between offenders, victims, and the community.[42]

Neurobiological Basis of Empathy and Reconciliation

Neuroscience research has provided valuable insights into the biological underpinnings of empathy, remorse, and reconciliation – key components of restorative justice processes:

1. **Mirror Neuron System:** Studies have shown that the mirror neuron system, which activates both when individuals perform actions and when they observe others performing the same actions, plays a crucial role in empathy and understanding others' emotions.[43]

---

41 Pragya Mishra, 'The Mindful Way to Freedom: An Enquiry into the Metaphysical Questions Bbehind Legal Responsibility' (2018) 60 *Journal of the Indian Law Institute* 332, 351.
42 Howard Zehr, *The Little Book of Restorative Justice: Revised and Updated* (Good Books 2015).
43 Giacomo Rizzolatti and Laila Craighero, 'The Mirror-Neuron System' (2004) 27 *Annual Review of Neuroscience* 169.

2. **Oxytocin and Trust:** Research has demonstrated that the hormone oxytocin enhances trust and cooperation, suggesting potential biochemical pathways for promoting reconciliation.[44]
3. **Neural Plasticity and Behavioral Change:** Understanding of neuroplasticity supports the potential for genuine behavioral change through restorative practices, even in individuals with longstanding patterns of antisocial behavior.[45]

These findings provide a scientific basis for the effectiveness of restorative justice approaches and suggest ways to enhance these practices through targeted interventions.

Integrating Neuroscience and Restorative Practices in India

In the Indian context, restorative justice principles resonate with traditional conflict resolution mechanisms such as Panchayats and Lok Adalats. A neuroscience-informed approach to restorative justice in India might involve:

1. **Neurofeedback in Victim–Offender Mediation:** Incorporating neurofeedback techniques to help participants regulate their emotional responses during mediation sessions.
2. **Mindfulness-Based Preparatory Programs:** Developing mindfulness training programs for both offenders and victims to enhance emotional regulation and empathy before engaging in restorative processes.
3. **Neuroimaging in Program Evaluation:** Using neuroimaging techniques to assess the effectiveness of restorative justice programs in promoting empathy and reducing aggressive tendencies.
4. **Culturally Informed Practices:** Integrating traditional Indian practices of reconciliation and conflict resolution with neuroscientific insights to create culturally resonant restorative justice models.

Neurolaw and Mental Health

The intersection of neuroscience, law, and mental health presents both challenges and opportunities for the Indian legal system. As our understanding of the neurobiological basis of mental disorders grows, it necessitates a reevaluation of how the law treats individuals with mental health conditions.

---

44 Paul J Zak, 'The Neuroscience of Trust' (2017) 95 *Harvard Business Review* 84.
45 Alvaro Pascual-Leone and others, 'The Plastic Human Brain Cortex' (2005) 28 *Annual Review of Neuroscience* 377.

Neuroscientific Insights into Mental Disorders

Recent neuroscientific research has provided new perspectives on mental disorders relevant to criminal behavior:

1. **Impulse Control Disorders:** Studies have shown altered activity in the prefrontal cortex and basal ganglia in individuals with impulse control disorders, suggesting a neurobiological basis for difficulties in behavioral inhibition.[46]
2. **Addiction:** Neuroimaging studies have revealed that substance addiction involves significant changes in brain structure and function, particularly in regions associated with reward processing and executive control.[47]
3. **Antisocial Personality Disorder:** Research has identified structural and functional brain differences in individuals with antisocial personality disorder, including reduced gray matter volume in regions associated with empathy and moral reasoning.[48]

These findings challenge simplistic notions of mental illness and criminal responsibility, suggesting a need for more nuanced legal approaches.

Reforming Mental Health Law in India

In light of these neuroscientific insights, several reforms to India's mental health laws and policies could be considered:

1. **Expanding the Insanity Defense:** Broadening the criteria for the insanity defense to include a wider range of neurocognitive impairments that may affect criminal responsibility
2. **Mental Health Courts:** Establishing specialized mental health courts that can better address the unique needs of offenders with mental health conditions, focusing on treatment and rehabilitation rather than punishment
3. **Neuropsychiatric Assessments:** Incorporating more comprehensive neuropsychiatric assessments into criminal proceedings to provide a more accurate picture of an offender's mental state and cognitive capacities
4. **Neurorehabilitation Programs:** Developing targeted neurorehabilitation programs for offenders with specific mental health conditions, based on the latest neuroscientific research.

A neurolaw-guided capacity framework would move beyond global, all-or-nothing determinations and adopt a more granular, ecological approach

---

46 Luke Clark, 'Disordered Gambling: The Evolving Concept of Behavioral Addiction' (2014) 1327 *Annals of the New York Academy of Sciences* 46.
47 Nora D Volkow and Marisela Morales, 'The Brain on Drugs: From Reward to Addiction' (2015) 162 *Cell* 712.
48 RJR Blair, 'The Neurobiology of Psychopathic Traits in Youths' (2013) 14 *Nature Reviews Neuroscience* 786.

that probes specific decision-making competencies across different domains and contexts.[49]

Neurolaw and Juvenile Justice

The application of neuroscientific insights to juvenile justice is particularly relevant in the Indian context, given the country's large youth population and ongoing debates about the appropriate age of criminal responsibility.

Neuroscience of Adolescent Brain Development

Neuroscientific research has provided crucial insights into adolescent brain development:

1. **Prefrontal Cortex Maturation:** Studies have shown that the prefrontal cortex, crucial for impulse control and decision-making, continues to develop well into early adulthood.[50]
2. **Reward Sensitivity:** Adolescents show heightened activation in brain regions associated with reward processing, potentially explaining increased risk-taking behavior.[51]
3. **Social Influence:** The adolescent brain is particularly sensitive to social influences, which can significantly impact decision-making and behavior.[52]

These findings suggest that adolescents may have diminished culpability for their actions compared to adults, due to their still developing cognitive control systems.

Implications for Indian Juvenile Justice

In light of these neuroscientific insights, several reforms to India's juvenile justice system could be considered:

1. **Age of Criminal Responsibility:** Reevaluating the appropriate age for full criminal responsibility, considering the extended period of brain development.

---

49 Pragya Mishra, 'The Mindful Way to Freedom: An Enquiry into the Metaphysical Questions behind Legal Responsibility' (2018) 60 *Journal of the Indian Law Institute* 332, 351.
50 BJ Casey, Rebecca M Jones and Todd A Hare, 'The Adolescent Brain' (2008) 1124 *Annals of the New York Academy of Sciences* 111.
51 Adriana Galvan and others, 'Earlier Development of the Accumbens Relative to Orbitofrontal Cortex Might Underlie Risk-Taking Behavior in Adolescents' (2006) 26 *Journal of Neuroscience* 6885.
52 Sarah-Jayne Blakemore and Kathryn L Mills, 'Is Adolescence a Sensitive Period for Sociocultural Processing?' (2014) 65 *Annual Review of Psychology* 187.

2. **Individualized Assessments:** Implementing more comprehensive, neuroscience-informed assessments of juvenile offenders to determine their level of cognitive maturity and capacity for rehabilitation.
3. **Developmentally Appropriate Interventions:** Designing rehabilitation programs that specifically target the developing adolescent brain, focusing on strengthening impulse control and decision-making skills.
4. **Education and Vocational Training:** Emphasizing education and skill development in juvenile justice programs, recognizing the heightened neuroplasticity of the adolescent brain.

Given the neuroscientific evidence on adolescent brain development, restorative approaches may be particularly effective for young offenders.[53]

Neurolaw and Legal Education

The emergence of neurolaw necessitates changes in legal education to prepare future lawyers, judges, and policymakers for the challenges and opportunities presented by neuroscience in the legal domain.

Integrating Neuroscience into Legal Curricula

Key areas for integration might include:

1. **Foundations of Neuroscience:** Providing law students with a basic understanding of brain structure and function relevant to legal issues.
2. **Neuroethics:** Exploring the ethical implications of neuroscientific advances in legal contexts.
3. **Neuroscientific Evidence:** Training in the interpretation and critical evaluation of neuroscientific evidence in legal proceedings.
4. **Interdisciplinary Collaboration:** Fostering partnerships between law schools and neuroscience departments to promote cross-disciplinary research and education.

Continuing Education for Legal Professionals

For practicing lawyers, judges, and policymakers, ongoing education in neurolaw could involve:

1. **Workshops and Seminars:** Regular training sessions on the latest developments in neuroscience relevant to law.
2. **Online Courses:** Developing accessible online resources for legal professionals to stay updated on neurolaw topics.

---

53 Pragya Mishra, 'The Mindful Way to Freedom: An Enquiry into the Metaphysical Questions behind Legal Responsibility' (2018) 60 *Journal of the Indian Law Institute* 332, 351.

3. **Judicial Training:** Incorporating neurolaw modules into judicial training programs to ensure judges are equipped to handle neuroscientific evidence in court.

The integration of neuroscience into Indian jurisprudence offers a transformative opportunity to create a more nuanced, effective, and humane legal system. By combining cutting-edge scientific insights with India's rich philosophical traditions, we can develop a uniquely Indian approach to neurolaw that respects both empirical evidence and cultural values.

This neuroscience-informed approach challenges us to reconsider fundamental concepts of free will, responsibility, and punishment. It pushes us toward a more compassionate understanding of human behavior, recognizing the complex interplay of biological, psychological, and social factors that contribute to criminal conduct.

At the same time, it offers new tools for prevention, rehabilitation, and justice, from neurofeedback-enhanced restorative practices to brain-based interventions for offenders. The potential for more targeted, effective interventions is immense, but so too are the ethical challenges we must navigate.

As we move forward, it will be crucial to maintain a balance between scientific progress and ethical considerations, ensuring that our evolving understanding of the brain enhances rather than diminishes human dignity and rights. We must be vigilant against the misuse of neurotechnology while remaining open to its potential benefits.

The path ahead is not without challenges. Integrating neuroscience into law will require significant changes in legal education, policy, and practice. It will demand interdisciplinary collaboration and a willingness to question long-held assumptions about human nature and justice.

Yet the potential rewards are profound. A neuroscience-informed legal system could be more effective in preventing crime, more successful in rehabilitating offenders, and more just in its treatment of all individuals. It could help us move beyond simplistic notions of punishment toward a more holistic approach to addressing the root causes of criminal behavior.

We are moving toward 'a neurocriminological wisdom of convolution and self-sculpting'"[54] – a perspective that recognizes the complexity of human behavior while affirming our capacity for growth and transformation. This emerging neurojurisprudence may well point the way toward a more enlightened approach to justice not just for India but for the global community.

As we stand at this intersection of neuroscience and law, we have the opportunity to pioneer a truly innovative approach to justice – one that is scientifically grounded, philosophically nuanced, and deeply humane. In doing so, we may not only transform our legal system but also deepen our understanding of what it means to be human in an age of rapid scientific advancement.

---

54 Pragya Mishra, 'The Mindful Way to Freedom: An Enquiry into the Metaphysical Questions Behindbehind Legal Responsibility' (2018) 60 *Journal of the Indian Law Institute* 332, 351.

8 Neurolaw and Mental Health Legislation in India

Analysis of India's Mental Health Laws from a Neurolaw Perspective

The intersection of neuroscience and mental health law represents a frontier in legal thought, challenging traditional notions of mental illness, capacity, and responsibility. In India, the Mental Healthcare Act of 2017 (MHCA) marked a significant step forward in mental health legislation, aligning the country's laws more closely with international human rights standards.[1] However, the rapid advancements in neuroscience necessitate a critical examination of this legislation through the lens of neurolaw.

Mental Healthcare Act 2017: An Overview

The MHCA 2017 replaced the outdated Mental Health Act of 1987, introducing several progressive features:

1. **Rights-Based approach:** The Act emphasizes the rights of persons with mental illness, including the right to access mental healthcare, the right to community living, and protection from cruel, inhuman, or degrading treatment.[2]
2. **Advance Directives:** The Act allows individuals to make advance directives specifying how they wish to be treated in the event of mental illness.[3]
3. **Decriminalization of Suicide:** The Act effectively decriminalizes suicide attempts, recognizing them as potential manifestations of mental illness requiring care and treatment rather than punishment.[4]

---

1 Mental Healthcare Act 2017.
2 Mental Healthcare Act 2017 s 18–28.
3 Mental Healthcare Act 2017 s 5–13.
4 Mental Healthcare Act 2017 s 115.

4. **Regulated Use of Electro-Convulsive Therapy (ECT):** The Act places restrictions on the use of ECT, particularly banning its unmodified form and its use in minors.[5]

While these provisions represent significant progress, examining them through a neuroscientific lens reveals both strengths and potential areas for improvement.

Neuroscientific Perspectives on Mental Illness

Recent neuroscientific research has challenged traditional categorical approaches to mental illness, suggesting instead a more dimensional view. Studies using neuroimaging techniques have revealed overlapping neural circuits implicated in various mental disorders, blurring the lines between diagnostic categories.[6]

This research has several implications for mental health law:

1. **Diagnostic Validity:** The neuroscientific evidence questions the validity of discrete diagnostic categories, suggesting a need for more nuanced legal approaches to mental illness.[7]
2. **Capacity Assessment:** Neuroscience offers new tools for assessing mental capacity, potentially providing more objective measures than traditional clinical assessments.[8]
3. **Treatment Efficacy:** Neuroimaging studies can provide insights into treatment efficacy, potentially informing legal decisions about involuntary treatment.[9]

Neurolaw Critique of the MHCA 2017

Examining the MHCA 2017 through a neurolaw lens reveals several areas where the Act may not fully align with current neuroscientific understanding:

1. **Binary Approach to Capacity:** The Act still largely operates on a binary notion of mental capacity, which may not reflect the nuanced,

---

5 Mental Healthcare Act 2017 s 95.
6 Thomas Insel and others, 'Research Domain Criteria (RDoC): Toward a New Classification Framework for Research on Mental Disorders' (2010) 167 *American Journal of Psychiatry* 748.
7 Steven E Hyman, 'The Diagnosis of Mental Disorders: The Problem of Reification' (2010) 11 *Annual Review of Clinical Psychology* 155.
8 Elyn R Saks and Dilip V Jeste, 'Capacity to Consent to or Refuse Treatment and/or Research: Theoretical Considerations' (2006) 24 *Behavioral Sciences & the Law* 411.
9 Helen S Mayberg and others, 'Deep Brain Stimulation for Treatment-Resistant Depression' (2005) 45 *Neuron* 651.

context-dependent nature of decision-making capacity revealed by neuroscience.[10]

2. **Limited Recognition of Neurodevelopmental Disorders:** While the Act's definition of mental illness is broad, it does not explicitly address neurodevelopmental disorders like autism spectrum disorders, which have significant implications for mental health and capacity.[11]

3. **Insufficient Integration of Neuroscientific Evidence:** The Act does not provide clear guidelines for the use of neuroscientific evidence in mental health proceedings, potentially missing opportunities for more informed decision-making.[12]

4. **Lack of Neuroplasticity Perspective:** The Act's approach to treatment and rehabilitation does not fully incorporate current understanding of neuroplasticity and the brain's capacity for change, which could inform more effective interventions.[13]

Mounting evidence from neuroscience challenges the efficacy of purely punitive approaches, suggesting that they may be counterproductive in reducing recidivism and promoting societal well-being.[14] This observation, while made in the context of criminal justice, is equally relevant to mental health law, where punitive or overly restrictive approaches may hinder recovery and reintegration.

Cultural Considerations in Indian Mental Health Law

Any analysis of Indian mental health law must consider the country's unique cultural context. Traditional Indian systems of medicine, such as Ayurveda, offer holistic approaches to mental health that may complement neuroscientific insights.[15] Moreover, the concept of the self in Indian philosophy, which often emphasizes interconnectedness over individualism, may have implications for how we conceptualize mental illness and treatment.[16]

The MHCA 2017 makes some efforts to recognize these cultural factors, for instance by including yoga and naturopathy under the definition of mental health professionals.[17] However, there is potential for further integration of culturally informed approaches with neuroscientific insights.

---

10 Elyn R Saks, 'Mental Capacity and the Law' in Jed Boardman, Geoff Dimock and Simon Shine (eds), *Oxford Textbook of Social Psychiatry* (Oxford University Press 2011).
11 Meng-Chuan Lai and others, 'Autism' (2014) 383 *The Lancet* 896.
12 Owen D Jones and others, 'Law and Neuroscience' (2013) 33 *Journal of Neuroscience* 17624.
13 Alvaro Pascual-Leone and others, 'The Plastic Human Brain Cortex' (2005) 28 *Annual Review of Neuroscience* 377.
14 Pragya Mishra, 'The Mindful Way to Freedom: An Enquiry into the Metaphysical Questions behind Legal Responsibility' (2018) 60 *Journal of the Indian Law Institute* 332, 337.
15 Chittaranjan Andrade and Rajiv Radhakrishnan, 'The Therapeutic Alliance and Neuroscience: Implications for Practice' (2009) 51 *Indian Journal of Psychiatry* 308.
16 Anand C Paranjpe, *Self and Identity in Modern Psychology and Indian Thought* (Springer Science & Business Media 2012).
17 Mental Healthcare Act (2017), s 2(1)(s).

Proposed Neuroscience-Informed Reforms

Based on the neurolaw analysis of the MHCA 2017, several reforms could be proposed to better align India's mental health legislation with current neuroscientific understanding.

Dimensional Approach to Mental Illness

Neuroscientific research suggests that mental disorders exist on a continuum rather than as discrete categories.[18] This understanding could inform legal reforms such as:

1. **Revised Definitions:** Updating the legal definition of mental illness to reflect a more dimensional view, recognizing varying degrees of impairment across different domains of functioning.
2. **Spectrum-Based Interventions:** Developing a more nuanced system of interventions that can be tailored to an individual's specific profile of cognitive and emotional functioning rather than broad diagnostic categories.
3. **Flexible Capacity Assessments:** Implementing capacity assessment tools that can capture the context-dependent nature of decision-making abilities, as revealed by neuroscience.[19]

Integration of Neuroscientific Evidence

The MHCA could be amended to explicitly recognize the role of neuroscientific evidence in mental health proceedings:

1. **Admissibility Guidelines:** Developing clear guidelines for the admissibility of neuroimaging and other neuroscientific evidence in mental health tribunals and courts
2. **Expert Testimony:** Establishing standards for expert testimony on neuroscientific matters in mental health cases
3. **Judicial Training:** Implementing training programs for judges and mental health review board members on interpreting neuroscientific evidence

Developing guidelines for the admissibility and interpretation of neuroscientific evidence related to an offender's mental state is crucial for the effective integration of neuroscience into legal decision-making.[20]

---

18 Thomas Insel and Bruce Cuthbert, 'Brain Disorders? Precisely' (2015) 348 *Science* 499.
19 Dilip V Jeste and others, 'Supported Decision Making in Serious Mental Illness' (2018) 81 *Psychiatry: Interpersonal and Biological Processes* 28.
20 Pragya Mishra, 'The Mindful Way to Freedom: An Enquiry into the Metaphysical Questions behind Legal Responsibility' (2018) 60 *Journal of the Indian Law Institute* 332, 337.

Neurodevelopmental Perspective

Incorporating a neurodevelopmental perspective into the MHCA could enhance its effectiveness in addressing the needs of individuals with neurodevelopmental disorders:

1. **Explicit Recognition:** Amending the Act to explicitly include neurodevelopmental disorders within its purview
2. **Developmental Trajectories:** Incorporating understanding of neurodevelopmental trajectories into treatment planning and capacity assessments
3. **Tailored Interventions:** Developing guidelines for interventions that are specifically tailored to the neurocognitive profiles of individuals with neurodevelopmental disorders

Neuroplasticity-Informed Rehabilitation

Neuroscientific insights into neuroplasticity could inform more effective rehabilitation approaches:

1. **Brain-Based Interventions:** Incorporating interventions that directly target neural circuits implicated in mental disorders, such as neurofeedback or transcranial magnetic stimulation[21]
2. **Cognitive Remediation:** Expanding the use of cognitive remediation therapies that leverage neuroplasticity to enhance cognitive functioning[22]
3. **Environmental Enrichment:** Developing guidelines for creating enriched environments in mental health facilities that promote positive neuroplastic changes[23]

Neuroethics Framework

As neuroscience plays an increasing role in mental health law, it is crucial to develop a robust neuroethics framework:

1. **Informed Consent:** Updating informed consent procedures to address the unique ethical issues raised by neurotechnological interventions

---

[21] Mark S George and others, 'Brain Stimulation for the Treatment of Psychiatric Disorders' (2007) 19 *Current Opinion in Psychiatry* 292.

[22] Til Wykes and others, 'A Meta-Analysis of Cognitive Remediation for Schizophrenia: Methodology and Effect Sizes' (2011) 168 *American Journal of Psychiatry* 472.

[23] DO Hebb, 'The Effects of Early Experience on Problem Solving at Maturity' (1947) 17 *American Psychologist* 306.

2. **Privacy Protections:** Developing stringent privacy protections for brain data collected in the course of mental health assessments or treatments
3. **Cognitive Liberty:** Explicitly recognizing the right to cognitive liberty – the freedom of individuals to control their own mental processes, cognition, and consciousness[24]

Developing comprehensive guidelines for the ethical use of neuroplasticity-based interventions in the criminal justice system is crucial.[25] This principle is equally applicable to mental health contexts.

Cultural Integration

Reforms should aim to better integrate culturally informed approaches with neuroscientific insights:

1. **Traditional Medicine:** Developing guidelines for the integration of traditional Indian medical approaches, such as Ayurveda and yoga, with neuroscience-based interventions
2. **Community-Based Care:** Expanding community-based care models that align with Indian cultural values of family and community support, informed by neuroscientific understanding of social influences on brain function[26]
3. **Culturally Adapted Assessments:** Developing and validating culturally appropriate neurocognitive assessment tools for use in Indian populations

Comparative Analysis with International Approaches

To fully appreciate India's unique position in the global neurolaw landscape and to contextualize the proposed reforms for India, it is crucial to examine how jurisdictions have incorporated neuroscientific insights into their mental health legislation. This comparative analysis will highlight both common challenges and distinctive approaches.

---

24 Jan Christoph Bublitz and Reinhard Merkel, 'Crimes against Minds: On Mental Manipulations, Harms and a Human Right to Mental Self-Determination' (2014) 8 *Criminal Law and Philosophy* 51.
25 Pragya Mishra, 'The Mindful Way to Freedom: An Enquiry into the Metaphysical Questions behind Legal Responsibility' (2018) 60 *Journal of the Indian Law Institute* 332, 337.
26 Vikram Patel and others, 'Effectiveness of an Intervention Led by Lay Health Counsellors for Depressive and Anxiety Disorders in Primary Care in Goa, India (MANAS): A Cluster Randomised Controlled Trial' (2010) 376 *The Lancet* 2086.

United States: The Neuroscience Revolution in Courts

The United States has been at the forefront of integrating neuroscientific evidence into legal proceedings. The landmark case of *Roper v. Simmons* (2005) saw the U.S. Supreme Court cite neuroscientific evidence on adolescent brain development to prohibit the death penalty for offenders under 18.[27] This decision marked a significant shift in how scientific evidence could influence legal reasoning at the highest level.

Subsequent cases, such as *Graham v. Florida* (2010) and *Miller v. Alabama* (2012), further extended this principle, demonstrating an increasing reliance on neuroscientific insights in judicial decision-making.[28] The U.S. approach is characterised by a relatively open attitude toward admitting neuroscientific evidence in court, albeit with ongoing debates about its proper interpretation and weight.

The United States has also seen significant integration of neuroscience into mental health law, particularly in the following areas:

1. **Neuroimaging in Court:** U.S. courts have increasingly admitted neuroimaging evidence in cases involving mental health issues, though with varying degrees of scepticism.[29]
2. **Neurodevelopmental Perspective:** The U.S. Supreme Court has cited neuroscientific evidence on adolescent brain development in several landmark cases involving juvenile offenders with mental health issues.[30]
3. **Mental Health Courts:** Many jurisdictions have established specialized mental health courts that aim to divert individuals with mental illness from the criminal justice system, often incorporating neuroscience-informed interventions.[31]

However, this enthusiastic embrace of neuroscience in law has also faced criticism. Some scholars argue that there is a risk of 'neuroexuberance' – an overreliance on neuroscientific evidence and biomedical models of mental illness, potentially neglecting social and environmental factors[32] without

---

27 *Roper v Simmons* (2005) 543 US 551.
28 Laurence Steinberg, 'The Influence of Neuroscience on US Supreme Court Decisions about Adolescents' Criminal Culpability' (2013) 14 *Nature Reviews Neuroscience* 513.
29 Owen D Jones and others, 'Neuroscientists in Court' (2013) 14 *Nature Reviews Neuroscience* 730.
30 Terry A Maroney, 'The False Promise of Adolescent Brain Science in Juvenile Justice' (2009) 85 *Notre Dame Law Review* 89.
31 Richard D Schneider, Hy Bloom and Mark Heerema, *Mental Health Courts: Decriminalizing the Mentally Ill* (Irwin Law 2007).
32 Nikolas Rose and Joelle M Abi-Rached, *Neuro: The New Brain Sciences and the Management of the Mind* (Princeton University Press 2013).

sufficient critical scrutiny.[33] This cautionary note is particularly relevant for India as it develops its own approach to neurolaw.

European Union: Cautious Integration and Ethical Frameworks

In contrast to the US, the European Union has adopted a more cautious approach to neurolaw. The emphasis in many EU countries has been on developing comprehensive ethical frameworks to guide the integration of neuroscience into legal systems.

For instance, the Netherlands has been pioneering in its approach, establishing the Netherlands Institute for Neuroscience to facilitate collaboration between neuroscientists and legal professionals.[34] This institute has been instrumental in developing guidelines for the use of neuroscientific evidence in Dutch courts, emphasising the need for rigorous scientific validation and ethical considerations.

The European approach is also characterized by a strong focus on privacy and data protection. The General Data Protection Regulation (GDPR) has significant implications for the collection and use of neuroscientific data in legal contexts, providing a model for balancing scientific advancement with individual rights.[35]

1. **Rights-Based Approach:** EU mental health policies strongly emphasize human rights, aligning with neuroscientific evidence on the importance of autonomy and social inclusion for mental well-being.[36]
2. **Dimensional Approach:** Some European countries, such as the Netherlands, have moved toward more dimensional approaches to mental health diagnosis and treatment, reflecting neuroscientific insights.[37]
3. **Neuroethics:** The EU has been at the forefront of developing neuroethics frameworks, with initiatives like the Human Brain Project dedicating significant resources to exploring the ethical implications of neuroscience.[38]

---

33 Stephen J Morse, 'Brain Overclaim Syndrome and Criminal Responsibility: A Diagnostic Note' (2006) 3 *Ohio State Journal of Criminal Law* 397.
34 Tade Matthias Spranger, *International Neurolaw: A Comparative Analysis* (Springer 2012).
35 Sjors Ligthart, 'Coercive Neuroimaging, Criminal Law, and Privacy: A European Perspective' (2019) 6 *Journal of Law and the Biosciences* 289.
36 Peter Bartlett, Oliver Lewis and Oliver Thorold, *Mental Disability and the European Convention on Human Rights* (Martinus Nijhoff Publishers 2007).
37 Jim van Os and others, 'Beyond DSM and ICD: Introducing "Precision Diagnosis" for Psychiatry Using Momentary Assessment Technology' (2013) 12 *World Psychiatry* 113.
38 Kathinka Evers, 'Neuroethics: A Philosophical Challenge' (2005) 6 *The American Journal of Bioethics* 31.

108 Neurolaw and Criminal Jurisprudence in India

Japan: Cultural Considerations in Neurolaw

Japan's approach to neurolaw offers valuable insights for India, given certain cultural similarities in their legal traditions. Japan has been particularly innovative in integrating neuroscientific insights into its juvenile justice system. The Japanese concept of shōnen (juvenile) in legal contexts has been influenced by neuroscientific evidence on adolescent brain development. This has led to more rehabilitative approaches for young offenders, resonating with the principle expressed in the ancient Indian text, *Hitopadesha*:

उपदेशो हि मूर्खाणां प्रकोपाय न शान्तये

(*Hitopadesha*, 1.5)

Mere advice to the unwise leads to anger, not peace.[39]

This wisdom aligns with the neuroscientific understanding that punitive approaches may be counterproductive for juvenile offenders, whose brains are still developing.

1. **Community-Based Care:** Japan has emphasized community-based care models, aligning with neuroscientific evidence on the importance of social support for mental health.[40]
2. **Culturally Informed Interventions:** Japanese mental health approaches often integrate cultural practices like Morita therapy, which has parallels with mindfulness-based interventions supported by neuroscience.[41]
3. **Neurotechnology Regulation:** Japan has been proactive in developing regulatory frameworks for neurotechnology, which could inform similar efforts in India.[42]

China: State-Driven Neurolaw Initiatives

China's approach to neurolaw is characterised by significant state involvement and investment. The Chinese government has funded large-scale research initiatives exploring the applications of neuroscience in law enforcement and the justice system.[43]

---

39 MR Kale, *Hitopadeśa* (Motilal Banarsidass 1967).
40 Tsuyoshi Akiyama and others, 'Mental Health Law in Japan: Recent Developments' (2019) 31 *International Journal of Law and Psychiatry* 101495.
41 David K Reynolds, *The Quiet Therapies: Japanese Pathways to Personal Growth* (University of Hawai'i Press 1980).
42 Nita A Farahany and others, 'The Ethics of Experimenting with Human Brain Tissue' (2018) 556 *Nature* 429.
43 Shen Fuxin, 'Neuroscience and Law in China' (2016) 2 *Journal of Law and the Biosciences* 459.

While this state-driven approach has led to rapid advancements, it has also raised concerns about privacy and the potential for misuse of neurotechnology. China's experience offers important lessons for India about the need to balance scientific progress with ethical considerations and individual rights.

Lessons for India

From this comparative analysis, several lessons emerge for India:

1. **Balanced Approach:** India could strive for a balance between the more neuroscience-embracing approach of the US and the more cautious, rights-focused approach of the EU.
2. **Cultural Integration:** Following Japan's example, India could further integrate its rich cultural traditions with neuroscientific insights in mental health law.
3. **Neuroethics Focus:** Drawing on EU initiatives, India could prioritize the development of a robust neuroethics framework to guide the integration of neuroscience into mental health law.
4. **Community Emphasis:** Building on its existing community-based approaches, India could further strengthen these models based on neuroscientific evidence of their efficacy.

India's Unique Position in Global Neurolaw

India's approach to neurolaw is uniquely positioned to draw from its rich philosophical traditions while engaging with cutting-edge neuroscience. This synthesis offers the potential for a distinctive contribution to global neurolaw discourse.

- **Integrating Spiritual Practices with Neuroscientific Rehabilitation:** India's ancient practices of yoga and meditation, now validated by neuroscientific research, offer promising avenues for offender rehabilitation. The principle underlying this approach is beautifully captured in the *Bhagavad Gita*:

उद्धरेदात्मनात्मानं नात्मानमवसादयेत्.

(Bhagavad Gita, 6.5)

Let a man raise himself by his own self; let him not debase himself.[44]

---

44 Eknath Easwaran, *The Bhagavad Gita* (2nd edn, Nilgiri Press 2007).

This integration of spiritual practices with neuroscience-informed rehabilitation could set a global precedent for holistic approaches to criminal justice.

- **Community-Based Approaches to Neurolaw: Lessons from Panchayati Raj:** India's tradition of community-based justice systems, exemplified by the Panchayati Raj, offers a unique perspective on how neurolaw principles could be applied at a grassroots level. This aligns with emerging neuroscientific understanding of the social brain and the importance of community in shaping behavior.[45]
- **Potential for Low-Cost Neurotechnology Solutions:** India's expertise in developing frugal innovations could be leveraged to create accessible neurotechnology solutions for legal applications. This could address the global challenge of making neurolaw approaches available in resource-constrained settings.

As India navigates its path in neurolaw, it has the opportunity to create a model that is scientifically rigorous, ethically sound, and culturally resonant. By learning from global experiences while drawing on its unique heritage, India can make a distinctive and valuable contribution to the evolving field of neurolaw.

Implementation Challenges and Strategies

While the proposed neuroscience-informed reforms offer significant potential benefits, their implementation in the Indian context would face several challenges:

Resource Constraints

India's healthcare system, particularly in mental health, faces significant resource constraints. Implementing neuroscience-based interventions and assessments may require substantial investment in equipment, training, and personnel.

Potential strategies to address this challenge include:

1. **Phased Implementation:** Introducing neuroscience-informed approaches gradually, starting with pilot programs in major urban centers.
2. **Public–Private Partnerships:** Collaborating with private sector entities to fund and implement neurotechnology in mental health care.

---

45 Michael Tomasello, 'The Ultra-Social Animal' (2014) 44 *European Journal of Social Psychology* 187.

3. **Task-Shifting:** Training nonspecialist health workers in basic neuroscience-informed interventions to extend reach in resource-limited settings.

Workforce Development

Implementing neuroscience-informed mental health care will require significant workforce development efforts.

Strategies could include:

1. **Curriculum Updates:** Revising medical and mental health professional curricula to incorporate more neuroscience content.
2. **Continuing Education:** Developing continuing education programs in neurolaw and mental health for legal and healthcare professionals.
3. **Interdisciplinary Training:** Creating interdisciplinary training programs that bring together legal professionals, mental health practitioners, and neuroscientists.

Cultural Acceptance

Integrating neuroscientific approaches into mental health care may face cultural resistance in some quarters.

Approaches to address this could include:

1. **Public Education:** Launching public awareness campaigns to educate the general public about neuroscience and mental health.
2. **Cultural Adaptation:** Ensuring that neuroscience-informed interventions are adapted to be culturally appropriate and respectful of local beliefs and practices.
3. **Stakeholder Engagement:** Involving community leaders, traditional healers, and religious figures in the development and implementation of neuroscience-informed mental health policies.

Legal and Ethical Challenges

The integration of neuroscience into mental health law raises complex legal and ethical issues that will need to be carefully navigated.

Strategies could include:

1. **Neuroethics Committees:** Establishing national and state-level neuroethics committees to provide guidance on ethical issues.

2. **Legal Framework Updates:** Systematically updating mental health and related laws to address neuroscience-specific issues like cognitive liberty and brain privacy.
3. **International Collaboration:** Engaging with international bodies and experts to draw on global best practices in neurolaw and mental health.

The integration of neuroscientific insights into India's mental health legislation offers a promising path toward more effective, humane, and scientifically grounded approaches to mental health care. By moving toward a more dimensional view of mental illness, incorporating neurodevelopmental perspectives, leveraging neuroplasticity in rehabilitation, and developing robust neuroethics frameworks, India has the opportunity to pioneer an innovative approach to mental health law.

However, this integration must be pursued thoughtfully, with careful consideration of resource constraints, workforce development needs, cultural factors, and ethical implications. By learning from international experiences while remaining grounded in its unique cultural context, India can develop a distinctively Indian approach to neurolaw in mental health.

We are moving toward 'a neurocriminological wisdom of convolution and self-sculpting'.[46] This perspective, applied to mental health law, suggests a future where legal frameworks recognize the complex, dynamic nature of mental health, and support interventions that leverage the brain's capacity for change and growth.

The path ahead is challenging but filled with potential. By embracing neuroscientific insights while remaining true to its cultural values and ethical principles, India has the opportunity to transform its approach to mental health care, potentially setting a model for other nations grappling with similar challenges. As this field continues to evolve, ongoing dialogue between neuroscientists, legal scholars, mental health professionals, policymakers, and the public will be crucial to ensure that advances in neuroscience translate into real improvements in mental health care and justice for all Indians.

---

46 Pragya Mishra, 'The Mindful Way to Freedom: An Enquiry into the Metaphysical Questions behind Legal Responsibility' (2018) 60 *Journal of the Indian Law Institute* 332, 337.

9 Neurotechnology and the Future of Criminal Justice

India and Beyond

Emerging Neurotechnologies and Their Potential Applications

The rapid advancement of neurotechnology is poised to revolutionize the field of criminal justice, offering new tools for investigation, assessment, and rehabilitation. As India and the global community grapple with the implications of these emerging technologies, it is crucial to examine their potential applications and the challenges they present.

Brain Imaging Technologies

Functional magnetic resonance imaging (fMRI) and other advanced brain imaging techniques have opened new avenues for understanding criminal behavior and assessing mental states.[1]

Potential Applications:

1. **Lie Detection:** While controversial, some researchers propose using fMRI as a more accurate alternative to traditional polygraph tests.[2]
2. **Mental State Assessment:** Brain imaging could potentially provide insights into an individual's mental state at the time of a crime, informing questions of criminal responsibility.[3]
3. **Risk Assessment:** Neuroimaging data might be used to assess an individual's likelihood of recidivism or violent behavior.[4]

---

1 Owen D Jones and others, 'Law and Neuroscience' (2013) 33 *Journal of Neuroscience* 17624.
2 Daniel D Langleben and others, 'Telling Truth from Lie in Individual Subjects with Fast Event-Related fMRI' (2005) 26 *Human Brain Mapping* 262.
3 Eyal Aharoni and others, 'Neuroprediction of Future Rearrest' (2013) 110 *Proceedings of the National Academy of Sciences* 6223.
4 Kent A Kiehl and others, 'Temporal Lobe Abnormalities in Semantic Processing by Criminal Psychopaths as Revealed by Functional Magnetic Resonance Imaging' (2004) 130 *Psychiatry Research: Neuroimaging* 297.

DOI: 10.4324/9781003567394-9

However, as cautioned, 'There is a risk that neuroimaging data could be collected, analysed, and used without their knowledge or consent, creating a new form of "neurosurveillance" that undermines the right to mental self-determination'.[5]

Brain–Computer Interfaces (BCIs)

BCIs allow direct communication between the brain and external devices, offering potential applications in both investigation and rehabilitation.[6]

Potential Applications:

1. **Memory Retrieval:** BCIs could potentially aid in retrieving memories relevant to criminal investigations.[7]
2. **Neurorehabilitation:** For offenders with neurological impairments, BCIs might assist in cognitive rehabilitation.[8]
3. **Thought-Based Communication:** In cases where individuals are unable to communicate verbally, BCIs could provide an alternative means of communication.[9]

Neurofeedback and Neuromodulation

These technologies allow for the monitoring and alteration of brain activity, offering potential tools for behavior modification and rehabilitation.[10]

Potential Applications:

1. **Impulse Control Training:** Neurofeedback could be used to help offenders improve their impulse control and emotional regulation.[11]

---

5 Pragya Mishra, 'The Mindful Way to Freedom: An Enquiry into the Metaphysical Questions behind Legal Responsibility' (2018) 60 *Journal of the Indian Law Institute* 332, 341.
6 Miguel Nicolelis, 'Brain-Machine Interfaces to Restore Motor Function and Probe Neural Circuits' (2003) 4 *Nature Reviews Neuroscience* 417.
7 Niels Birbaumer and Leonardo G Cohen, 'Brain-Computer Interfaces: Communication and Restoration of Movement in Paralysis' (2007) 579(3) *Journal of Physiology* 621, DOI: 10.1113/jphysiol.2006.125633.
8 Niels Birbaumer and Leonardo G Cohen, 'Brain-Computer Interfaces: Communication and Restoration of Movement in Paralysis' (2007) 579 *The Journal of Physiology* 621.
9 Jonathan R Wolpaw and others, 'Brain-Computer Interfaces for Communication and Control' (2002) 113 *Clinical Neurophys*
10 Ranganatha Sitaram and others, 'Closed-Loop Brain Training: The Science of Neurofeedback' (2017) 18 *Nature Reviews Neuroscience* 86.
11 Robert T Thibault and others, 'Neurofeedback, Self-Regulation, and Brain Imaging: Clinical Science and Fad in the Service of Mental Disorders' (2015) 57 *Psychotherapy and Psychosomatics* 314.

2. **Addiction Treatment:** Neuromodulation techniques like transcranial magnetic stimulation (TMS) show promise in treating addiction, a common factor in criminal behavior.[12]
3. **Aggression Management:** These technologies could potentially be used to help individuals manage aggressive tendencies.[13]

Predictive Algorithms and AI

The integration of neuroscientific data with artificial intelligence could lead to more sophisticated predictive tools in criminal justice.[14]

Potential Applications:

1. **Risk Assessment:** AI algorithms incorporating neuroscientific data could potentially provide more accurate predictions of recidivism risk.[15]
2. **Early Intervention:** Predictive tools might identify individuals at risk of criminal behavior, allowing for early intervention.[16]
3. **Personalized Rehabilitation:** AI could help tailor rehabilitation programs based on an individual's neurocognitive profile.[17]

Pharmacological Interventions

Advancements in neuropharmacology offer potential new approaches to managing criminal behavior.[18]

Potential Applications:

1. **Impulse Control:** Medications targeting specific neurotransmitter systems could potentially help manage impulsive behavior.[19]

---

12 Vaughn R Steele and others, 'Machine Learning of Brain Structure and Function in Substance Use Disorders' (2019) 15 *Neuropsychopharmacology* 1.
13 Nora D Volkow and others, 'Addiction: Decreased Reward Sensitivity and Increased Expectation Sensitivity Conspire to Overwhelm the Brain's Control Circuit' (2010) 32 *BioEssays* 748.
14 Richard Berk and others, 'Fairness in Criminal Justice Risk Assessments: The State of the Art' (2018) 50 *Sociological Methods & Research* 3.
15 Eyal Aharoni and others, 'Predictive Accuracy in the Neuroprediction of Rearrest' (2014) 9 *Social Neuroscience* 332.
16 Adrian Raine, *The Anatomy of Violence: The Biological Roots of Crime* (Pantheon Books 2013).
17 Russell A Poldrack and others, 'Predicting Violent Behavior: What Can Neuroscience Add?' (2018) 22 *Trends in Cognitive Sciences* 111.
18 Trevor Robbins and Bita Moghaddam, 'Neuropharmacology: A Reductionist Approach to Understanding the Brain' (2017) 40 Annual Review of Pharmacology and Toxicology 489.
19 Alan A Baumeister and others, 'The Direct and Indirect Effects of Dopamine on Impulsivity' (2020) 10 *Frontiers in Psychiatry* 244.

2. **Cognitive Enhancement:** Drugs that enhance cognitive function might be used as part of rehabilitation programs.[20]
3. **Mood Regulation:** Pharmacological interventions could help manage mood disorders that contribute to criminal behavior.[21]

As these technologies continue to evolve, their potential applications in criminal justice are likely to expand. However, their use raises significant ethical and legal challenges that must be carefully considered.

Ethical and Legal Challenges in the Indian and Global Context

The integration of neurotechnology into criminal justice systems presents a myriad of ethical and legal challenges, many of which are particularly acute in the Indian context.

Privacy and Mental Freedom

The use of neurotechnology in criminal justice raises profound questions about mental privacy and cognitive liberty.[22]

Key Challenges:

1. **Brain Data Privacy:** How can we protect the privacy of brain data collected through neurotechnological means?
2. **Cognitive Liberty:** Does the use of neurotechnology in criminal investigations infringe on an individual's right to mental self-determination?
3. **Informed Consent:** How can meaningful informed consent be obtained for the use of neurotechnology, particularly in the coercive context of criminal justice?

In the Indian context, where the right to privacy has only recently been recognized as a fundamental right,[23] these issues take on added significance. Ensuring

---

20 Barbara J Sahakian and Sharon Morein-Zamir, 'Neuroethical Issues in Cognitive Enhancement' (2011) 33 *Journal of Psychopharmacology* 559.
21 Nora D Volkov, 'Personalizing the Treatment of Substance Use Disorders' (2020) 177 *American Journal of Psychiatry* 113.
22 Jan Christoph Bublitz and Reinhard Merkel, 'Crimes against Minds: On Mental Manipulations, Harms and a Human Right to Mental Self-Determination' (2014) 8 *Criminal Law and Philosophy* 51.
23 *Justice KS Puttaswamy, (Retd) v Union of India* [2017] 10 SCC 1 (Supreme Court of India).

that neuroplasticity-based interventions respect individual autonomy and do not amount to forced 'brain change' is a crucial ethical consideration.[24]

Reliability and Validity of Neurotechnological Evidence

The use of neurotechnological evidence in legal proceedings raises questions about its reliability and validity.[25]

Key Challenges:

1. **Scientific Validity:** How can we ensure that neurotechnological evidence meets rigorous scientific standards?
2. **Interpretation of Data:** How can complex neuroscientific data be accurately interpreted in legal contexts?
3. **Cultural Bias:** How might cultural factors influence the interpretation of neuroscientific data, particularly in a diverse society like India?

Equal Access and Social Justice

The introduction of neurotechnology into criminal justice systems raises concerns about equity and social justice.[26]

Key Challenges:

1. **Access to Technology:** How can we ensure equal access to neurotechnological assessments and interventions across different socioeconomic groups?
2. **Bias in Algorithms:** How can we prevent bias in AI algorithms that incorporate neuroscientific data?
3. **Cultural Sensitivity:** How can neurotechnological approaches be adapted to be culturally appropriate in diverse contexts like India?

Autonomy and Rehabilitation

The use of neurotechnology in rehabilitation raises questions about autonomy and the nature of punishment.[27]

---

24 Pragya Mishra, 'The Mindful Way to Freedom: An Enquiry into the Metaphysical Questions behind Legal Responsibility' (2018) 60 *Journal of the Indian Law Institute* 332, 341.
25 Owen D Jones and others, 'Neuroscientists in Court' (2013) 14 *Nature Reviews Neuroscience* 730.
26 Jennifer A Chandler, 'The Use of Neuroscientific Evidence in Canadian Criminal Proceedings' (2015) 2 *Journal of Law and the Biosciences* 550.
27 Nicole A Vincent, 'Neurolaw and Direct Brain Interventions' (2014) 8 *Criminal Law and Philosophy* 43.

Key Challenges:

1. **Voluntary Participation**: How can we ensure that participation in neurotechnology-based rehabilitation programs is truly voluntary?
2. **Changing Personality**: Do neurointerventions that alter brain function impinge on an individual's autonomy and identity?
3. **Balancing Punishment and Treatment**: How can we balance the punitive aspects of criminal justice with neurotechnology-based rehabilitation approaches?

Predictive Justice and Free Will

The use of neurotechnology in predictive justice raises fundamental questions about free will and determinism.[28]

Key Challenges:

1. **Philosophical Implications**: How do predictive neurotechnologies challenge our notions of free will and moral responsibility?
2. **Preemptive Intervention**: Is it ethical to intervene based on neurotechnological predictions of future criminal behavior?
3. **Stigmatization**: How can we prevent the stigmatization of individuals based on their neurotechnological profiles?

These challenges are particularly complex in the Indian context, where diverse philosophical traditions offer varying perspectives on free will and determinism. As Mishra observes, 'The Buddhist concept of anatta (non-self) and the Advaita Vedanta notion of the illusory nature of the ego bear striking parallels to neuroscientific findings about the distributed and emergent nature of consciousness'.[29]

Developing a Regulatory Framework for Neurotechnology in Criminal Justice

Given the profound implications of neurotechnology in criminal justice, developing a comprehensive regulatory framework is crucial. This framework must balance the potential benefits of these technologies with the need to protect individual rights and societal values.

---

28 Stephen J Morse, 'Criminal Law and Common Sense: An Essay on the Perils and Promise of Neuroscience' (2015) 99 *Marquette Law Review* 39.

29 Pragya Mishra, 'The Mindful Way to Freedom: An Enquiry into the Metaphysical Questions behind Legal Responsibility' (2018) 60 *Journal of the Indian Law Institute* 332, 341.

Principles for a Regulatory Framework

Any regulatory framework for neurotechnology in criminal justice should be guided by key principles:

1. **Human Rights Protection:** Ensuring that the use of neurotechnology does not infringe on fundamental human rights, including privacy, dignity, and cognitive liberty[30]
2. **Scientific Validity:** Establishing rigorous standards for the scientific validity and reliability of neurotechnological evidence[31]
3. **Ethical Use:** Ensuring that neurotechnology is used ethically, with due consideration for individual autonomy and societal impact[32]
4. **Equity and Nondiscrimination:** Preventing the discriminatory use of neurotechnology and ensuring equal access to its benefits[33]
5. **Transparency and Accountability:** Ensuring transparency in the development and use of neurotechnology and establishing clear accountability mechanisms[34]

Key Components of a Regulatory Framework

1. **Legal and Ethical Oversight**

   - Establishing a national neuroethics committee to provide guidance on ethical issues related to neurotechnology in criminal justice.
   - Developing specific legislation to govern the use of neurotechnology in criminal justice contexts.
   - Creating judicial guidelines for the admissibility and interpretation of neurotechnological evidence.

2. **Standards and Protocols**

   - Developing technical standards for neurotechnology used in criminal justice settings
   - Establishing protocols for the collection, storage, and use of brain data
   - Creating guidelines for the integration of neurotechnological assessments in legal proceedings

---

30 Marcello Ienca and Roberto Andorno, 'Towards New Human Rights in the Age of Neuroscience and Neurotechnology' (2017) 13 *Life Sciences, Society and Policy* 5.
31 Stephen J Morse and William T Newsome, 'Criminal Responsibility, Criminal Competence, and Prediction of Criminal Behavior' in Stephen J Morse and Adina L Roskies (eds), *A Primer on Criminal Law and Neuroscience* (Oxford University Press 2013).
32 Judy Illes and others, 'Neurotalk: Improving the Communication of Neuroscience Research' (2010) 11 *Nature Reviews Neuroscience* 61.
33 Teneille Brown and Emily Murphy, 'Through a Scanner Darkly: Functional Neuroimaging as Evidence of a Criminal Defendant's Past Mental States' (2010) 62 *Stanford Law Review* 1119.
34 Henry T Greely, 'Neuroscience, Mindreading, and the Courts: The Example of Pain' (2015) 18 *Journal of Health Care Law & Policy* 171.

3. **Consent and Privacy Protection**
   - Developing robust informed consent procedures for the use of neurotechnology in criminal justice contexts
   - Establishing stringent privacy protections for brain data, including regulations on data storage, access, and sharing
   - Creating mechanisms for individuals to access and challenge their own brain data

4. **Training and Education**
   - Developing training programs for legal professionals, law enforcement, and correctional staff on the use and interpretation of neurotechnology
   - Implementing public education initiatives to increase understanding of neurotechnology and its implications for criminal justice

5. **Research and Development**
   - Establishing ethical guidelines for neurotechnology research in criminal justice contexts
   - Promoting interdisciplinary research collaborations among neuroscientists, legal scholars, and ethicists
   - Funding research on the long-term impacts of neurotechnology use in criminal justice

6. **International Cooperation**
   - Engaging in international dialogue and cooperation on the regulation of neurotechnology in criminal justice
   - Harmonizing Indian regulations with international standards and best practices

Challenges in Implementing a Regulatory Framework

Implementing a comprehensive regulatory framework for neurotechnology in criminal justice faces several challenges, particularly in the Indian context:

1. **Resource Constraints:** India's criminal justice system already faces significant resource constraints. Implementing and enforcing a new regulatory framework for neurotechnology will require substantial investment in infrastructure, training, and personnel.

Potential Solutions:

- Phased implementation of regulations, starting with pilot programs in major urban centers

- Public–private partnerships to fund the necessary infrastructure and training
- Leveraging existing regulatory bodies and mechanisms to reduce costs

2. **Technological Disparities:** The uneven distribution of technological resources across India could lead to disparities in the application of neurotechnology in criminal justice.

Potential Solutions:

- Developing mobile neurotechnology units to serve remote areas
- Implementing telemedicine-style approaches for neurotechnological assessments
- Prioritizing the development of low-cost, portable neurotechnology solutions

3. **Cultural and Social Factors:** India's diverse cultural landscape presents challenges in implementing a uniform regulatory framework for neurotechnology.

Potential Solutions:

- Engaging with community leaders and local stakeholders in the development of regulations
- Incorporating cultural sensitivity training into neurotechnology education programs
- Developing culturally adapted versions of neurotechnological assessments and interventions

4. **Legal System Readiness:** India's legal system may not be fully prepared to handle the complex issues raised by neurotechnology.

Potential Solutions:

- Establishing specialized courts or tribunals to handle cases involving neurotechnology
- Implementing comprehensive training programs for judges and lawyers on neurotechnology
- Developing a cadre of court-appointed neurotechnology experts

5. **Ethical Dilemmas:** The use of neurotechnology in criminal justice raises profound ethical questions that may not have clear answers.

Potential Solutions:

- Establishing a national neuroethics advisory board to provide ongoing guidance
- Promoting public dialogue and debate on the ethical implications of neurotechnology in criminal justice
- Incorporating ethics education into all neurotechnology training programs

The Way Forward: A Roadmap for India

Developing a comprehensive regulatory framework for neurotechnology in criminal justice is a complex, long-term endeavor. For India, a phased approach might be most practical:

Phase 1: Groundwork and Capacity Building (1–3 years)

- Establish a national task force on neurotechnology in criminal justice.
- Conduct a comprehensive review of existing laws and regulations relevant to neurotechnology.
- Initiate public awareness and education campaigns.
- Begin developing training programs for legal and criminal justice professionals.

Phase 2: Initial Regulation and Pilot Implementation (3–5 years)

- Draft and pass initial legislation governing the use of neurotechnology in criminal justice.
- Establish a national neuroethics committee.
- Implement pilot programs for neurotechnology use in select jurisdictions.
- Develop preliminary standards and protocols for neurotechnology use.

Phase 3: Comprehensive Implementation and Refinement (5–10 years)

- Fully implement the regulatory framework nationwide.
- Establish specialized neurotechnology courts or tribunals.
- Refine regulations based on pilot program outcomes and emerging technologies.
- Engage in international collaboration and knowledge sharing.

Throughout this process, it will be crucial to maintain flexibility and adaptability, as the field of neurotechnology is rapidly evolving. Regular review and updating of the regulatory framework will be necessary to keep pace with technological advancements and emerging ethical challenges.

India's Potential Contributions to Global Neurolaw

India's unique blend of ancient wisdom and modern scientific prowess positions it to make significant contributions to the global neurolaw discourse.

This section explores three key areas where India's approach could influence and enrich international perspectives on neurolaw.

Frugal Innovation in Neurotechnology for Legal Applications

India's renowned capacity for frugal innovation, colloquially known as jugaad, could revolutionize the accessibility of neurotechnology in legal contexts. This approach resonates with the ancient Indian principle of aparigraha, or non-possessiveness, which encourages doing more with less:

यथोपजोषं विषयान् प्रतिपद्येत कामतः।
आपः प्रविश्य तिष्ठेत कूर्मोऽङ्गानीव सर्वशः॥

(Bhagavad Gita, 2.58)

One who is able to withdraw his senses from sense objects, as the tortoise draws its limbs within the shell, is firmly fixed in perfect consciousness.[35]

This philosophy, when applied to neurotechnology, could lead to the development of cost-effective, portable neuroimaging devices and user-friendly neuroassessment tools. For instance, Indian researchers have already made strides in developing low-cost EEG devices for brain–computer interfaces.[36] Such innovations could democratise access to neurotechnology, making neurolaw approaches feasible even in resource-constrained settings.

Moreover, India's robust information technology sector could contribute to developing sophisticated yet affordable AI-driven algorithms for analyzing neuroscientific data in legal contexts. This could potentially address the global challenge of interpreting complex brain data in courtrooms, making neurolaw more accessible and applicable worldwide.

Holistic Models of Neurorehabilitation: Combining Modern Science and Traditional Practices

India's holistic approach to health and well-being, rooted in ancient systems like Ayurveda and Yoga, offers a unique perspective on neurorehabilitation. This approach aligns with the Ayurvedic principle of treating the whole person, not just the symptoms:

सुखार्थाः सर्वभूतानां मताः सर्वाः प्रवृत्तयः।
सुखं च न विना धर्मात् तस्माद्धर्मपरो भवेत्॥

('Charaka Samhita', Sutrasthana 1.15)

---

35 Eknath Easwaran, *The Bhagavad Gita* (2nd edn, Nilgiri Press 2007).
36 Rajesh Singla and others, 'Soft Computing Based Portable and Wearable EEG Devices for Neurological Health Care' (2020) 11 *Frontiers in Neuroscience* 1.

124 *Neurolaw and Criminal Jurisprudence in India*

All beings strive for happiness. There is no happiness without righteousness. Therefore, one should live a righteous life.[37]

By integrating traditional practices like meditation and yoga with modern neuroscience-informed interventions, India could pioneer comprehensive neurorehabilitation programs for offenders. Recent studies have shown that mindfulness practices can induce neuroplastic changes in brain regions associated with self-regulation and empathy.[38]

A uniquely Indian model of neurorehabilitation might combine:

1. Mindfulness-based cognitive therapy
2. Yoga and pranayama for stress reduction and impulse control
3. Ayurvedic lifestyle recommendations for balanced mental health
4. Modern cognitive training techniques
5. Community reintegration practices inspired by traditional social structures

Such a holistic approach could address not only the neurobiological factors contributing to criminal behavior but also the broader psychosocial and spiritual dimensions of rehabilitation.

Ethical Frameworks Informed by Dharmic Traditions

India's dharmic traditions offer rich resources for developing ethical frameworks to guide the application of neuroscience in law. The concept of dharma, which encompasses duty, righteousness, and cosmic order, provides a nuanced perspective on individual and societal responsibilities:

धर्मो रक्षति रक्षितः

(Manu Smriti, 8.15)

Dharma protected, protects.[39]

This principle could inform a neuroethics framework that balances individual rights with societal well-being. For instance, in addressing the use of neurotechnology for crime prediction, an Indian ethical framework might emphasize:

1. Respect for cognitive liberty (drawing from the concept of sva-dharma, or individual duty).

---

37 PV Sharma, *Caraka-Samhita: Text with English Translation* (Chaukhambha Orientalia 2014).
38 Yi-Yuan Tang and others, 'The Neuroscience of Mindfulness Meditation' (2015) 16 *Nature Reviews Neuroscience* 213.
39 Patrick Olivelle, *Manu's Code of Law: A Critical Edition and Translation of the Mānava-Dharmaśāstra* (Oxford University Press 2005).

2. Fairness and nondiscrimination (inspired by the principle of samata, or equanimity).
3. Transparency and accountability (reflecting the value of satya, or truthfulness).
4. Rehabilitation over punishment (embodying ahimsa, or nonviolence).

Such a framework could offer a more holistic and compassionate approach to neurolaw ethics, potentially influencing global discussions on the ethical implications of neuroscience in legal contexts.

Furthermore, India's tradition of philosophical debate and synthesis could contribute to resolving apparent conflicts between deterministic neuroscientific findings and legal concepts of responsibility. The Advaita Vedanta concept of viveka (discernment) might offer insights into how to navigate the complex relationship between brain states and behavior in legal decision-making.

By leveraging these unique strengths – frugal innovation, holistic rehabilitation models, and ethically rich philosophical traditions – India has the potential to make distinctive and valuable contributions to the global neurolaw discourse. As neuroscience continues to reshape our understanding of human behavior and responsibility, India's approach could offer a model for integrating scientific rigor with ethical depth and cultural wisdom, potentially leading to more just and effective legal systems worldwide.

The integration of neurotechnology into criminal justice systems presents both unprecedented opportunities and profound challenges. For India, navigating this complex landscape will require a delicate balance between embracing the potential benefits of these technologies and safeguarding fundamental rights and ethical principles.

We are moving toward 'a neurocriminological wisdom of convolution and self-sculpting'.[40] This perspective suggests a future where our understanding of criminal behavior and our approaches to justice are deeply informed by neuroscientific insights, while still recognizing the complexity and plasticity of the human brain and mind.

The development of a comprehensive regulatory framework for neurotechnology in criminal justice is not just a legal or technical challenge but a profound societal one. It will require ongoing dialogue between scientists, legal scholars, policymakers, ethicists, and the public. Moreover, it will necessitate a reimagining of core concepts in criminal justice, from culpability and punishment to rehabilitation and reform.

As India embarks on this journey, it has the opportunity to pioneer a uniquely Indian approach to neurolaw – one that draws on its rich philosophical traditions, respects its cultural diversity, and addresses its specific social and economic realities. By doing so, India could not only transform its own

---

40 Pragya Mishra, 'The Mindful Way to Freedom: An Enquiry into the Metaphysical Questions behind Legal Responsibility' (2018) 60 *Journal of the Indian Law Institute* 332, 341.

criminal justice system but also contribute valuable insights to the global discourse on neurotechnology and law.

The path ahead is challenging, but it is also filled with potential. By approaching these challenges with wisdom, foresight, and a commitment to justice and human dignity, India can help shape a future where neurotechnology serves as a tool for creating a more just, humane, and effective criminal justice system.

10 Toward an Indian Neurojuridical Ontology
India's Contributions to Global Neurolaw

Synthesis of Key Insights

As we stand at the intersection of neuroscience and law, it is crucial to synthesize the key insights that have emerged from our exploration of neurolaw in the Indian context. Our journey has revealed the transformative potential of neuroscience in reshaping India's criminal justice system, while also highlighting the unique contributions that India's rich philosophical and cultural heritage can make to the global discourse on neurolaw. This synthesis will form the foundation for developing a distinctly Indian approach to neurolaw and identifying India's potential contributions to the global discourse.

The Neuroscientific Challenge to Traditional Legal Concepts

Throughout our examination, we have seen how neuroscientific findings challenge traditional legal concepts, particularly in the realm of criminal law. Key insights include:

1. **Free Will and Responsibility:** Neuroscientific research has problematized simplistic notions of free will, suggesting a more nuanced understanding of human agency and responsibility.[1] If our actions are the result of unconscious neural processes, to what extent can we be said to have voluntary control over our behavior?[2]
2. **Mental States and Culpability:** Brain imaging studies have provided new insights into mental states relevant to criminal behavior, challenging traditional legal approaches to assessing culpability.[3]

---

1 Michael S Gazzaniga, 'The Law and Neuroscience' (2008) 60 *Neuron* 412.
2 Pragya Mishra, 'The Mindful Way to Freedom: An Enquiry into the Metaphysical Questions behind Legal Responsibility' (2018) 60 *Journal of the Indian Law Institute* 332, 337.
3 Owen D Jones and others, 'Law and Neuroscience' (2013) 33 *Journal of Neuroscience* 17624.

3. **Capacity and Competence:** Neuroscience offers new tools for assessing mental capacity and competence, potentially leading to more accurate and fair legal determinations.[4]

Promise and Perils of Neurotechnology

Our exploration has revealed both the potential benefits and risks associated with the integration of neurotechnology into the legal system:

1. **Enhanced Assessment:** Neurotechnological tools offer the potential for more accurate assessment of mental states, risk, and capacity.[5]
2. **Novel Rehabilitation Approaches:** Neuroscience-informed interventions present new possibilities for offender rehabilitation and behavior modification.[6]
3. **Privacy and Autonomy Concerns:** The use of neurotechnology in legal contexts raises significant concerns about mental privacy and cognitive liberty.[7]

Cultural and Philosophical Considerations

A key insight from our exploration is the importance of cultural and philosophical perspectives in shaping neurolaw:

1. **Indian Philosophical Traditions:** Concepts from Indian philosophy, such as the Buddhist notion of anatta (non-self) and the Advaita Vedanta understanding of consciousness, offer unique perspectives on neuroscientific findings.[8]
2. **Holistic Approaches:** Traditional Indian approaches to mental health and well-being, such as yoga and Ayurveda, provide complementary frameworks for understanding the mind–brain relationship.[9]

---

4 Stephen J Morse and William T Newsome, 'Criminal Responsibility, Criminal Competence, and Prediction of Criminal Behavior' in Stephen J Morse and Adina L Roskies (eds), *A Primer on Criminal Law and Neuroscience* (Oxford University Press 2013).
5 Kent A Kiehl and others, 'Temporal Lobe Abnormalities in Semantic Processing by Criminal Psychopaths as Revealed by Functional Magnetic Resonance Imaging' (2004) 130 *Psychiatry Research: Neuroimaging* 297.
6 R Serin and others, 'Correctional Programs' in DP Farrington and others (eds), *Springer Series on Evidence-Based Crime Policy* (Springer 2019).
7 Nita A Farahany, 'Incriminating Thoughts' (2012) 64 *Stanford Law Review* 351.
8 Evan Thompson, *Waking, Dreaming, Being: Self and Consciousness in Neuroscience, Meditation, and Philosophy* (Columbia University Press 2014).
9 BN Gangadhar and others, 'Yoga and Mental Health Services' (2013) 55 *Indian Journal of Psychiatry* S224.

Toward an Indian Neurojuridical Ontology   129

3. **Cultural Diversity:** India's cultural diversity necessitates a nuanced approach to neurolaw that can accommodate varying cultural perspectives on mind, responsibility, and justice.[10]

Ethical and Legal Frameworks

Our examination has highlighted the need for robust ethical and legal frameworks to guide the development of neurolaw:

1. **Neuroethics:** The development of a comprehensive neuroethics framework is crucial for addressing the ethical challenges posed by neuroscience in law.[11]
2. **Legal Adaptations:** Existing legal frameworks, particularly in criminal law, need to be adapted to incorporate neuroscientific insights.[12]
3. **Human Rights Considerations:** The integration of neuroscience into law must be guided by a strong commitment to human rights, including the right to mental privacy and cognitive liberty.[13]

A Distinctly Indian Approach to Neurolaw

Building on these key insights, we can now outline the contours of a distinctly Indian approach to neurolaw. This approach should be grounded in India's unique cultural, philosophical, and legal traditions while engaging with global neuroscientific and legal developments.

Integration of Indian Philosophical Perspectives

A distinctly Indian neurolaw should draw upon the rich philosophical traditions of the subcontinent:

1. **Non-Dual Consciousness:** The Advaita Vedanta concept of non-dual consciousness (advaita) offers a framework for understanding the relationship between brain and mind that aligns with some contemporary neuroscientific theories.[14]

---

10 Suparna Choudhury and Jan Slaby (eds), *Critical Neuroscience: A Handbook of the Social and Cultural Contexts of Neuroscience* (Wiley-Blackwell 2012).
11 Judy Illes and others, 'Neurotalk: Improving the Communication of Neuroscience Research' (2010) 11 *Nature Reviews Neuroscience* 61.
12 Stephen J Morse, 'Criminal Law and Common Sense: An Essay on the Perils and Promise of Neuroscience' (2015) 99 *Marquette Law Review* 39.
13 Marcello Ienca and Roberto Andorno, 'Towards New Human Rights in the Age of Neuroscience and Neurotechnology' (2017) 13 *Life Sciences, Society and Policy* 5.
14 Anand C Paranjpe, *Self and Identity in Modern Psychology and Indian Thought* (Springer Science & Business Media 2012).

2. **Karmic Responsibility:** The Buddhist and Hindu notions of karma provide a nuanced perspective on responsibility that could inform legal approaches to culpability.[15]
3. **Mindfulness and Self-Regulation:** The emphasis on mindfulness and self-awareness in Indian contemplative traditions aligns with neuroscientific research on cognitive control and emotion regulation.[16]

As an archer aims an arrow, a carpenter carves wood, the wise shapes their life –Dhammapad[17]

By focusing on wholesome thoughts and directing them we can influence and shape the plasticity of our brains beneficially.

— *Dr. Richard Davidson[18]*

The convergence of statements of an ancient Buddhist Scripture and a world-renowned neuroscientist represents not merely a theoretical reconciliation of science and spirituality but is instead the result of a series of experiments led by Dr. Davidson in cooperation with the Dalai Lama on the effects of meditation on the brain.[19]

Holistic Approach to Mental Health and Rehabilitation

India's traditional systems of medicine and well-being offer holistic approaches that could be integrated with neuroscientific insights:

1. **Yoga and Neuroscience:** The integration of yoga practices with neuroscience-informed interventions could offer unique approaches to offender rehabilitation.[20]
2. **Ayurvedic Perspectives:** Ayurvedic understanding of mind–body types (doshas) could inform personalized approaches to assessment and treatment in legal contexts.[21]

---

15 Chakravarthi Ram-Prasad, *Indian Philosophy and the Consequences of Knowledge: Themes in Ethics, Metaphysics and Soteriology* (Ashgate 2007).
16 Yi-Yuan Tang and others, 'The Neuroscience of Mindfulness Meditation' (2015) 16 *Nature Reviews Neuroscience* 213.
17 Gil Fronsdal (tr), *The Dhammapada: A New Translation of the Buddhist Classic with Annotations* (verse 33, Shambhala 2006).
18 Richard J Davidson and Daniel Goleman, *Altered Traits: Science Reveals How Meditation Changes Your Mind, Brain, and Body* (Avery 2017) 87.
19 Pragya Mishra, 'The Mindful Way to Freedom: An Enquiry into the Metaphysical Questions behind Legal Responsibility' (2018) 60 *Journal of the Indian Law Institute* 332, 337.
20 Sat Bir S Khalsa, 'Yoga as a Therapeutic Intervention' in Gerald Zaltman and others (eds), *Complementary and Alternative Therapies Research* (American Psychological Association 2008).
21 Bhushan Patwardhan, 'Bridging Ayurveda with Evidence-based Scientific Approaches in Medicine' (2014) 5 *EPMA Journal* 19.

3. **Community-Based Approaches:** Drawing on India's strong traditions of community support, neurolaw interventions could be designed to involve families and communities in rehabilitation efforts.[22]

Cultural Sensitivity in Neuroscientific Assessment

Given India's cultural diversity, a distinctly Indian neurolaw must be culturally sensitive:

1. **Culturally Adapted Assessments:** Neurocognitive assessments used in legal contexts should be adapted and validated for India's diverse populations.[23]
2. **Diverse Normative Standards:** The interpretation of neurobiological data should consider diverse cultural norms and practices.[24]
3. **Language Considerations:** Given India's linguistic diversity, neurolaw approaches should be developed and implemented in multiple languages.[25]

Technology-Enabled Access to Justice

India's growing technological capabilities could be leveraged to enhance access to neuroscience-informed justice:

1. **Mobile Neurotechnology:** Development of portable, low-cost neurotechnology solutions could enhance access to neuroscience-informed assessments in remote areas.[26]
2. **AI-Assisted Interpretation:** Artificial intelligence could be used to assist in the interpretation of complex neuroscientific data in legal contexts, making it more accessible to judges and lawyers.[27]
3. **Telemedicine Approaches:** Telemedicine models could be adapted for neuroscience-informed legal assessments, increasing access in underserved areas.[28]

---

22 Vikram Patel and others, 'Effectiveness of an Intervention Led by Lay Health Counsellors for Depressive and Anxiety Disorders in Primary Care in Goa, India (MANAS): A Cluster Randomised Controlled Trial' (2010) 376 *The Lancet* 2086.
23 Urvakhsh Meherwan Mehta and others, 'Cultural Neuroscience and Psychopathology: Prospects for Cultural Psychiatry' (2011) 35 *Trends in Cognitive Sciences* 219.
24 Joan Y Chiao and others, 'Cultural Neuroscience: Progress and Promise' (2013) 7 *Psychological Inquiry* 1.
25 Loraine K Obler and Deborah Fein (eds), *The Exceptional Brain: Neuropsychology of Talent and Special Abilities* (Guilford Press 1988).
26 Thomas R Insel and others, 'Digital Phenotyping: Technology for a New Science of Behavior' (2017) 318 JAMA 1215.
27 Nikolaos Koutsoupias, 'Artificial Intelligence in Forensic Science and Law' (2021) 3 *International Journal of Law and Information Technology* 1.
28 Jayashree Dasgupta and others, 'Bridging the Digital Divide: Telemedicine and Education for Mental Health Professionals in Developing Countries' in Nitesh V Chawla and Stefano Boccaletti (eds), *Advances in Network Science* (Springer 2020).

Rights-Based Framework

A distinctly Indian neurolaw should be grounded in a strong rights-based framework:

1. **Right to Cognitive Liberty:** Recognizing and protecting the right to cognitive liberty as an extension of the fundamental right to privacy.[29]
2. **Right to Neurorehabilitation:** Establishing a right to access neuroscience-informed rehabilitation as part of the right to health.[30]
3. **Protection against Neurodiscrimination:** Developing legal safeguards against discrimination based on neurocognitive profiles.[31]

India's Potential Contributions to Global Neurolaw Discourse

India, with its unique blend of ancient wisdom and modern scientific prowess, is well positioned to make significant contributions to the global neurolaw discourse.

Integrative Models of Mind and Consciousness

India's philosophical traditions offer sophisticated models of mind and consciousness that could enrich global neurolaw discourse:

1. **Nonreductive Approaches:** Indian philosophical concepts like Chit (pure consciousness) from Vedanta philosophy offer non-reductive approaches to understanding consciousness, potentially informing legal concepts of mental states.[32]
2. **Embodied Cognition:** The emphasis on embodied practices in Indian traditions aligns with contemporary neuroscientific theories of embodied cognition, offering new perspectives on the mind–body relationship relevant to law.[33]

---

29 Jan Christoph Bublitz and Reinhard Merkel, 'Crimes against Minds: On Mental Manipulations, Harms and a Human Right to Mental Self-Determination' (2014) 8 *Criminal Law and Philosophy* 51.
30 Jennifer A Chandler, 'Autonomy and the Unintended Legal Consequences of Emerging Neurotherapies' (2013) 6 *Neuroethics* 249.
31 Gregor Wolbring and Lucy Diep, 'The Discussions around Precision Genetic Engineering: Role of and Impact on Disabled People' (2016) 5 *Laws* 37.
32 B Alan Wallace, *Contemplative Science: Where Buddhism and Neuroscience Converge* (Columbia University Press 2007).
33 Evan Thompson, *Mind in Life: Biology, Phenomenology, and the Sciences of Mind* (Harvard University Press 2007).

3. **Meditative Insights:** The deep insights into the nature of mind derived from Indian meditative traditions could inform global understanding of cognitive processes relevant to legal decision-making.[34]

Holistic Rehabilitation Models

India's holistic approaches to health and well-being could contribute to global discussions on offender rehabilitation:

1. **Mind–Body Interventions:** India could pioneer the integration of mind–body practices like yoga and meditation with neuroscience-informed rehabilitation programs.[35]
2. **Community-Based Rehabilitation:** Drawing on its strong community structures, India could develop models of community-based neurorehabilitation that could be adapted globally.[36]
3. **Personalized Interventions:** Ayurvedic approaches to personalized medicine could inform the development of individualized neurorehabilitation programs.[37]

Ethical Frameworks for Neurolaw

India's rich tradition of ethical thought could contribute to the development of global neuroethical frameworks:

1. **Dharmic Ethics:** The concept of dharma, emphasizing duty and cosmic order, could offer new perspectives on neuroethical issues.[38]
2. **Non-Harm (Ahimsa):** The principle of non-harm, central to many Indian philosophical traditions, could inform ethical guidelines for neurotechnological interventions.[39]
3. **Collective Well-Being:** Indian ethical traditions emphasizing collective well-being could contribute to discussions on balancing individual rights with societal interests in neurolaw.[40]

---

34 Antoine Lutz and others, 'Attention Regulation and Monitoring in Meditation' (2008) 12 *Trends in Cognitive Sciences* 163.
35 Shirley Telles and others, 'Research on Traditional Meditation, Mindfulness and Yoga: A Scientometric Analysis' (2018) 9 *Frontiers in Psychology* 3.
36 Athena Demertzi and others, 'Looking for the Self in Pathological Unconsciousness' (2013) 7 *Frontiers in Human Neuroscience* 538.
37 Bhushan Patwardhan and others, 'Ayurveda and Natural Products Drug Discovery' (2008) 12 *Current Science* 1.
38 Roy W Perrett, *Hindu Ethics: A Philosophical Study* (University of Hawai'i Press 1998).
39 Christopher Key Chapple, *Nonviolence to Animals, Earth, and Self in Asian Traditions* (SUNY Press 1993).
40 Amartya Sen, *The Idea of Justice* (Harvard University Press 2009).

134 Neurolaw and Criminal Jurisprudence in India

Cultural Diversity in Neurolaw

India's experience in managing cultural diversity could inform global approaches to culturally sensitive neurolaw:

1. **Multicultural Assessment Models:** India could develop models for neurocognitive assessment that account for cultural diversity, potentially applicable in other multicultural societies.[41]
2. **Cultural Competence in Neurolaw:** India's experience could inform global efforts to develop cultural competence in the application of neuroscience to law.[42]
3. **Diverse Philosophical Perspectives:** India's engagement with diverse philosophical traditions could model how different cultural perspectives can be integrated into neurolaw frameworks.[43]

Technological Innovations

India's growing technological capabilities could contribute to global neurolaw in several ways:

1. **Affordable Neurotechnology:** India could lead in developing low-cost, scalable neurotechnologies for use in legal contexts, potentially benefiting resource-limited jurisdictions globally.[44]
2. **AI in Neurolaw:** India's expertise in artificial intelligence could contribute to the development of AI tools for interpreting neuroscientific data in legal contexts.[45]
3. **Mobile Neurolaw Solutions**: India's experience with mobile technologies could inform the development of mobile platforms for neuroscience-informed legal assessments.[46]

---

41 Jyotsna Agnihotri Gupta and Anjan Mukherjee, 'Biotechnology and the Idea of Justice in India' (2014) 7 *Asian Biotechnology and Development Review* 35.
42 Suparna Choudhury and others, 'Critical Neuroscience: Linking Neuroscience and Society through Critical Practice' (2009) 4 *BioSocieties* 61.
43 Jonardon Ganeri, *The Concealed Art of the Soul: Theories of Self and Practices of Truth in Indian Ethics and Epistemology* (Oxford University Press 2007).
44 Nita A Farahany and others, 'The Ethics of Experimenting with Human Brain Tissue' (2018) 556 *Nature* 429.
45 Amit Ray, *Compassionate Artificial Intelligence: Frameworks and Algorithms* (Compassionate AI Lab 2018).
46 Rajendra Gupta and others, 'Digital India: Transforming India into a Knowledge Economy' (2019) 14 *IT Professional* 24.

Legal Innovations

India's legal system, with its unique blend of common law heritage and indigenous legal traditions, could contribute novel approaches to neurolaw:

1. **Alternative Dispute Resolution:** India's experience with alternative dispute resolution mechanisms could inform the development of neuroscience-informed mediation and restorative justice practices.[47]
2. **Public Interest Litigation:** India's robust public interest litigation tradition could be leveraged to address neuroethical issues and promote cognitive rights.[48]
3. **Integrative Jurisprudence:** India could pioneer an integrative jurisprudence that synthesizes neuroscientific insights with traditional legal principles and cultural values.[49]

Challenges and Future Directions

While the potential of neurolaw in India is immense, several challenges must be addressed:

1. **Resource Constraints:** Implementing neuroscience-based approaches in India's overburdened justice system will require significant investment and creative solutions.
2. **Capacity Building:** There is a pressing need for interdisciplinary training programs to equip legal professionals, neuroscientists, and policymakers with the necessary skills to navigate this emerging field.
3. **Cultural Acceptance:** Efforts must be made to build public understanding and acceptance of neuroscience-based approaches in the justice system.
4. **Ethical Vigilance:** As neurotechnology advances, constant ethical scrutiny and public dialogue will be crucial to prevent misuse and protect individual rights.

Future Research Priorities

1. Longitudinal studies on the efficacy of neuroscience-informed interventions in the Indian context
2. Development of culturally adapted neurocognitive assessment tools

---

47 Upendra Baxi, 'Access to Justice in a Globalized Economy: Some Reflections' in S Tilak (ed), *Understanding Social Justice* (Social Science Press 2013).
48 SP Sathe, *Judicial Activism in India: Transgressing Borders and Enforcing Limits* (Oxford University Press 2002).
49 Rajeev Bhargava, *The Promise of India's Secular Democracy* (Oxford University Press 2010).

3. Exploration of the intersection between artificial intelligence, neuroscience, and law in India
4. Investigation of the neurobiology of crime in the Indian population, considering unique genetic and environmental factors

A Call to Action

As we stand at the cusp of a neuroscientific revolution in law, India has the opportunity to lead the way in developing a more humane, effective, and scientifically grounded approach to criminal justice. This endeavor will require the concerted efforts of various stakeholders:

- **Legal Professionals:** Embrace neuroscientific insights and integrate them into legal practice and jurisprudence.
- **Policymakers:** Develop forward-thinking policies that facilitate the responsible integration of neuroscience into the justice system.
- **Neuroscientists:** Engage in interdisciplinary dialogue and conduct research that addresses the specific needs of the Indian legal context.
- **Ethicists and Philosophers:** Help develop robust ethical frameworks that respect India's cultural diversity while upholding universal human rights.
- **Educators:** Create interdisciplinary curricula that prepare the next generation of professionals to work at the intersection of neuroscience and law.
- **Civil Society:** Engage in public discourse about the implications of neurolaw and hold institutions accountable for ethical implementation.

As we stand at the cusp of a neuroscientific revolution in law, India is uniquely positioned to make significant contributions to the global neurolaw discourse. By synthesizing its rich philosophical traditions, cultural diversity, and growing scientific capabilities, India can offer a distinctly holistic and humane approach to neurolaw.

The development of an Indian neurojuridical ontology presents both challenges and opportunities. It requires a delicate balance between embracing neuroscientific insights and preserving core cultural values and ethical principles. It demands a willingness to question long-held legal assumptions while remaining true to the fundamental tenets of justice and human dignity.

We are moving toward 'a neurocriminological wisdom of convolution and self-sculpting'.[50] This perspective, rooted in both ancient Indian wisdom and cutting-edge neuroscience, offers a promising path forward. It suggests a future where our legal systems are informed by a deep understanding of the human mind and brain, yet remain grounded in ethical principles and cultural wisdom.

---

50 Pragya Mishra, 'The Mindful Way to Freedom: An Enquiry into the Metaphysical Questions behind Legal Responsibility' (2018) 60 *Journal of the Indian Law Institute* 332, 337.

The journey toward this future will require ongoing dialogue among neuroscientists, legal scholars, ethicists, policymakers, and the public. It will necessitate interdisciplinary collaboration and cross-cultural exchange. Most importantly, it will require a commitment to using neuroscientific insights to create more just, humane, and effective legal systems.

As India continues to develop its approach to neurolaw, it has the potential not only to transform its own legal landscape but also to make profound contributions to the global discourse on neuroscience and law. By offering a unique perspective that bridges ancient wisdom and modern science, India can help shape a future where neurolaw serves as a tool for enhancing justice, promoting rehabilitation, and upholding human dignity.

In this endeavor, India can draw inspiration from its own philosophical traditions. As the ancient text *Bhagavad Gita* reminds us, 'योगस्थ: कुरु कर्माणि' (Yogasthah kuru karmani) – 'Established in Yoga, perform action'.[51] In the context of neurolaw, this wisdom calls us to ground our actions in deep understanding (yoga) while actively engaging with the challenges at hand.

As we embark on this transformative journey, let us seize the opportunity to forge a neurolaw framework that harmonizes scientific rigor with ethical integrity and cultural sensitivity. India stands poised to make an indelible mark on the global landscape of justice in this neuroscientific era. Moving forward, we must approach this monumental task with a blend of ancient wisdom and modern insight, infusing our efforts with compassion, and an unwavering commitment to justice. By working in concert, we can sculpt a legal system that not only reflects our deepening understanding of the human mind and behavior but that also upholds the timeless values of dignity and fairness. In this endeavor, we have the potential not only to revolutionize India's legal paradigm but also to illuminate new paths in the global pursuit of a more enlightened, effective, and humane approach to justice.

---

51 *Bhagavad Gita*, Chapter 2, Verse 48.

Glossary

Anatta: In Buddhist philosophy, the doctrine of non-self or the absence of a permanent, unchanging self.
Cognitive Liberty: The right to mental self-determination, including the freedom to control one's own cognitive processes.
Dharma: In Indian philosophy, the eternal law of the cosmos, inherent in the very nature of things.
fMRI (Functional Magnetic Resonance Imaging): A neuroimaging technique that measures brain activity by detecting changes in blood oxygenation and flow.
Mens Rea: The mental element of a crime; the intent to commit a crime.
Neurocriminology: The application of neuroscience to understand, predict, and prevent criminal behavior.
Neurofeedback: A type of biofeedback that uses real-time displays of brain activity to teach self-regulation of brain function.
Neurolaw: The interdisciplinary field that examines the implications and applications of neuroscience in legal contexts.
Neuroplasticity: The brain's ability to reorganize itself by forming new neural connections throughout life.
Vipassana: A meditation technique that involves observing one's physical sensations and mental events in a nonreactive way.

Appendices

Appendix A: Overview of Key Brain Structures and Their Functions in Relation to Criminal Behavior

1. **Prefrontal Cortex:**
   - Function: Executive control, decision-making, impulse control
   - Relevance: Dysfunction linked to impulsivity and poor judgment in criminal behavior
2. **Amygdala:**
   - Function: Emotional processing, fear response
   - Relevance: Abnormalities associated with psychopathy and aggressive behavior
3. **Hippocampus:**
   - Function: Memory formation and consolidation
   - Relevance: Implicated in stress-related disorders and PTSD in offenders
4. **Anterior Cingulate Cortex:**
   - Function: Error detection, conflict monitoring
   - Relevance: Reduced activity observed in individuals with antisocial behavior
5. **Nucleus Accumbens:**
   - Function: Reward processing
   - Relevance: Involved in addiction and impulsive behaviors

Appendix B: Summary of Major Neuroscientific Studies Relevant to Criminal Law

1. **Libet et al. (1983)** – 'Time of conscious intention to act in relation to onset of cerebral activity'
   - **Key finding:** Brain activity precedes conscious decision to act.

2. **Raine et al. (2000)** – 'Reduced prefrontal gray matter volume and reduced autonomic activity in antisocial personality disorder'
   - **Key finding:** Structural brain differences in individuals with antisocial personality disorder

3. **Greene et al. (2001)** – 'An fMRI investigation of emotional engagement in moral judgment'
   - **Key finding:** Different brain regions activated for personal and impersonal moral dilemmas

4. **Aharoni et al. (2013)** – 'Neuroprediction of future rearrest'
   - **Key finding:** Brain activity in the anterior cingulate cortex predicts likelihood of rearrest.

5. **Pardini et al. (2014)** – 'Lower amygdala volume in men is associated with childhood aggression, early psychopathic traits, and future violence.'
   - **Key finding:** Amygdala volume linked to aggressive behavior and violence

Appendix C: Comparison of Neurolaw Approaches in Different Countries

1. **United States:**
   - Extensive use of neuroscientific evidence in courts
   - Landmark cases incorporating neuroscience (e.g., *Roper v. Simmons*)
   - Active research programs in universities and institutes

2. **United Kingdom:**
   - More cautious approach to neuroscientific evidence
   - Focus on mental health applications
   - Royal Society report on 'Neuroscience and the Law' (2011)

3. **Netherlands:**
   - Pioneer in integrating neuroscience into the legal system
   - Netherlands Institute for Neuroscience collaborates with legal institutions
   - Research on neurolaw and juvenile justice

4. **Japan:**
   - Emphasis on neuroscientific research for crime prevention
   - Integration of neurofeedback in some rehabilitation programs
   - Cultural considerations in applying Western neurolaw concepts
5. **India:**
   - Emerging field with potential for unique contributions
   - Integration of traditional practices (e.g., yoga, meditation) with neuroscience
   - Challenges in resource allocation and implementation

Appendix D: Sample Neuroscience-Informed Rehabilitation Program Outline

1. **Assessment Phase:**
   - Neuropsychological testing
   - Brain imaging (if available)
   - Psychological and behavioral assessments

2. **Individualized Treatment Plan:**
   - Cognitive-behavioral therapy
   - Mindfulness-based stress reduction
   - Neurofeedback sessions (if available)

3. **Skill-Building Modules:**
   - Emotional regulation training
   - Impulse control exercises
   - Decision-making workshops

4. **Physical Health Component:**
   - Nutrition education
   - Exercise regimen
   - Sleep hygiene training

5. **Social Reintegration Preparation:**
   - Family therapy sessions
   - Vocational training
   - Community service projects

6. **Ongoing Monitoring and Support:**
   - Regular progress assessments
   - Gradual reduction of program intensity
   - Post-release follow-up plan

Appendix E: Ethical Guidelines for the Use of Neurotechnology in Legal Contexts

1. **Informed Consent:**
   - Full disclosure of the nature and purpose of neurotechnological interventions
   - Explanation in clear, nontechnical language
   - Right to refuse without negative consequences

2. **Privacy and Data Protection:**
   - Strict protocols for handling brain data
   - Limited access to authorized personnel only
   - Secure storage and eventual destruction of data

3. **Nondiscrimination:**
   - Prohibit use of neurotechnology for discriminatory purposes
   - Ensure equal access to neurotechnology-based interventions

4. **Reliability and Validity:**
   - Use of only scientifically validated neurotechnologies
   - Regular review and updating of technologies and methodologies

5. **Limits of Interpretation:**
   - Clear guidelines on what can and cannot be inferred from neurotechnological data
   - Prohibition of using neurotechnology for mind-reading or thought policing

6. **Right to Mental Integrity:**
   - Protect individuals' right to cognitive liberty
   - Prohibit coerced use of neurotechnology

7. **Oversight and Accountability:**
   - Establish review boards for neurotechnology use in legal contexts
   - Regular audits and public reporting

8. **Continuous Education:**
   - Mandatory training for legal professionals on neurotechnology
   - Public education initiatives on neurolaw

Statement: The definitions and explanations provided in the glossary and appendices are original and formulated based on my independent research and analysis. They are derived from an integration of established neuroscientific concepts and their application within the context of criminal behavior and legal principles. Each entry is carefully constructed to reflect my interpretation of relevant literature, studies, and real-world cases as they relate to the field of neurolaw.

Bibliography

Aharoni E, GM Vincent, CL Harenski, VD Calhoun, W Sinnott-Armstrong, MS Gazzaniga, KA Kiehl, 'Neuroprediction of Future Rearrest' (2013) 110 Proceedings of the National Academy of Sciences 6223.

Baskin-Sommers R and Fonteneau K, 'Correctional Change through Neuroscience' (2016) 85 Fordham Law Review 423.

Blair RJR, 'The Neurobiology of Psychopathic Traits in Youths' (2013) 14(11) Nature Reviews Neuroscience 786–799.

Chandler JA, 'The Use of Neuroscientific Evidence in Canadian Criminal Proceedings' (2018) 5(2) Journal of Law and the Biosciences 550–579.

Farahany NA, 'Incriminating Thoughts' (2012) 64 Stanford Law Review 351.

Greene J and Cohen J, 'For the Law, Neuroscience Changes Nothing and Everything' (2004) 359(1451) Philosophical Transactions of the Royal Society of London B: Biological Sciences 1775–1785.

Greene JD, RB Sommerville, LE Nystrom, JM Darley, JD Cohen, 'An fMRI Investigation of Emotional Engagement in Moral Judgment' (2001) 293 Science 2105.

Jones OD, Schall JD and Shen FX, 'Law and Neuroscience' (2013) 33(45) Journal of Neuroscience 17624–17630.

Libet B, CA Gleason, EW Wright, DK Pearl, 'Time of Conscious Intention to Act in Relation to Onset of Cerebral Activity' (1983) 106 Brain 623.

Mishra P, 'The Mindful Way to Freedom: An Enquiry into the Metaphysical Questions behind Legal Responsibility' (2018) 60(3) Journal of the Indian Law Institute 332–352.

Morse SJ, 'Criminal Law and Common Sense: An Essay on the Perils and Promise of Neuroscience' (2015) 99 Marquette Law Review 39.

Pardini DA, A Raine, K Erickson, R Loeber, 'Lower Amygdala Volume in Men is Associated with Childhood Aggression, Early Psychopathic Traits, and Future Violence' (2014) 72 Biological Psychiatry 64.

Raine A, T Lencz, S Bihrle, L LaCasse, P Colletti, 'Reduced Prefrontal Gray Matter Volume and Reduced Autonomic Activity in Antisocial Personality Disorder' (2000) 57 Archives of General Psychiatry 119.

Raine A, *The Anatomy of Violence: The Biological Roots of Crime* (Vintage 2013).

Tang YY, Hölzel BK and Posner MI, 'The Neuroscience of Mindfulness Meditation' (2015) 16(4) Nature Reviews Neuroscience 213–225.

Index

addiction: brain disease model of 30–31; drug policy and 29–31; neurobiology of 96; treatment approaches 60, 115
adolescent brain development: criminal responsibility and 29, 97–98; judicial recognition of 32–33; neuroscience of 97; policy implications 97–98
advance directives: implementation challenges 102; in Mental Healthcare Act 100–101
Artificial Intelligence (AI): in criminal justice 115; ethical considerations 117–118; predictive algorithms 115; risk assessment tools 115
autonomy: cognitive liberty and 117; mental health law and 102; neuroethical considerations 117–118; in rehabilitation 117–118
ayurveda: holistic approaches 63–64; mind-body connection 63–64; neuroscience integration 63–64

Bharatiya Nyaya Sanhita (BNS): analysis through neuroscientific lens 26–28; mens rea concept in 26–27; proposed reforms 35–38; sentencing provisions 31
Brain-Computer Interfaces (BCIs): applications in criminal justice 114; ethical considerations 116–117; technological developments 114

brain imaging: admissibility in courts 24–25; ethical considerations 116–117; legal applications 113–114; limitations of 117
buddhist philosophy: anatta concept 90–91; cognitive science and 62–63; mindfulness practices 62–63

capacity assessment: cultural considerations 131; mental health law and 101–102; neuroscientific approaches 101; reforms needed 103
cognitive liberty: definition 116; legal protection of 132; neurotechnology and 116–117; privacy concerns 116
community-based approaches: cultural integration 131; rehabilitation programs 59–60; restorative justice 49–50
criminal responsibility: free will debate 83–85; mental illness and 27–28; neuroscientific challenges to 85–87; philosophical perspectives 87–91
cultural considerations: assessment protocols 131; neurolaw implementation 131; rehabilitation approaches 131; traditional practices 130–131

Index 145

determinism: compatibility with responsibility 84–85; Indian philosophical perspectives 91–93; neuroscientific evidence for 83–84
drug policy: addiction treatment 30–31; international approaches 33–34; neuroscience-informed reforms 30–31

ethical considerations: cognitive liberty 116–117; data privacy 116; neurotechnology use 116–118; rehabilitation programs 78–79
evidence, neuroscientific: admissibility standards 24–25; case studies 39–41; international approaches 32–35; reliability concerns 117

free will: compatibilist perspectives 76–77; Indian philosophical views 91–93; neuroscientific challenges to 83–85; responsibility and 85–87

human rights: cognitive liberty as 132; mental health law and 100–101; neuroethics and 89; neurotechnology impacts on 116–117

Indian philosophy: consciousness concepts 129–130; karma theory 91–92; mind-body connection 63–64; neurolaw integration 87–89

juvenile justice: adolescent brain development 97–98; international approaches 32–33; neuroscience implications 28–29; reforms needed 97–98

legal education: neurolaw curriculum 98–99; professional training needs 98–99

mental health: legislation analysis 100–103; neuroscience integration 95–97; proposed reforms 103–105; traditional approaches 63–64
Mental Healthcare Act 2017: analysis of 100–102; neurolaw critique 101–102; proposed reforms 103–105
mindfulness: neuroscience of 62–63; rehabilitation applications 47; Vipassana meditation 69–72

neuroimaging: admissibility issues 24–25; ethical considerations 116–117; legal applications 113–114; limitations of 117
neuroplasticity: criminal rehabilitation and 55–57; evidence for 56–57; implications for law 57–59; types relevant to rehabilitation 56
neurotechnology: emerging developments 113–115; ethical challenges 116–118; legal applications 113–115; regulatory framework 118–122

predictive justice: AI applications 115; ethical concerns 118; limitations of 118; risk assessment tools 115
privacy: brain data protection 116; cognitive liberty and 116–117; ethical considerations 116; regulatory needs 119

rehabilitation: community-based approaches 59–60; neuroscience-informed models 45–48; traditional practices integration 60–61; Vipassana meditation program 69–72
restorative justice: cultural considerations 49–50; neuroscientific basis 48–49; traditional practices and 49–50; victim-offender mediation 49

sentencing: neuroscience-informed approaches 43–45; proposed reforms 42–43; punitive vs. rehabilitative models 43–44

146 *Index*

technology: artificial intelligence applications 115; brain-computer interfaces 114; emerging developments 113–115; ethical considerations 116–118
traditional practices: Ayurveda integration 63–64; meditation techniques 62–63; rehabilitation applications 60–61; yoga applications 63

vipassana meditation: implementation in prisons 69–72; neuroscientific evidence 70–72; prison program case study 69–82; rehabilitation outcomes 74–76

yoga: cognitive flexibility and 63; neuroscience integration 63; rehabilitation applications 63–64; traditional practices 63

Made in the USA
Columbia, SC
29 December 2024

b684ab9f-1691-461e-a0f6-8098b8cd3a0aR01